Joachim Klang • Tim Bischoff • Philipp Honvehlmann

LEGO TIPS, TRICKS, AND BUILDING TECHNIQUES

THE BIG UNOFFICIAL LEGO BUILDERS BOOK

HEEL

ACKNOWLEDGEMENT

Thanks to some pioneers and revolutionaries, some of whom we know in person and admire:

2LegoOrNot2Lego	DecoJim	Jojo	markus19840420	Sirens-Of-Titan
Arvo Brothers	- Derfel Cadarn -	Karwik	marshal banana	Spencer_R
ArzLan	Digger1221	Kat	McBricker	T.Oechsner
Bart Willen	Eastpole77	Lazer Blade	Mijasper	Taz-Maniac
Ben®	Fianat	lego_nabii	Misterzumbi	ted @ndes
Brian Corredor	Fraslund	Legohaulic	Nannan Z	TheBrickAvenger
Bricksonwheels	Fredoichi	LEGOLAS	NENN	Théolego
Brickthing	Gabe Umland	Legonardo Davidy	Ochre Jelly	tnickolaus
Bricktrix	Gambort	Legopard	„Orion Pax"	Toltomeja
Bruceywan	gearcs	Legotrucks	Paul Vermeesch	x_Speed
captainsmog	Henrik Hoexbroe	_lichtblau_	Pepa Quin	Xenomurphy
Cole Blaq	Homa	‚LL'	RoccoB	
Cuahchic	Joe Meno	Mark of Falworth	Sir Nadroj	

Particular thanks are due to Uwe Kurth, Christian Treczoks, Eugen Sellin, and Jonas Kramm for their enthusiastic support, and to Lutz Uhlmann for drawing up the construction guidelines. We're also grateful to mijasper and Xenomurphy for allowing us to use their creations. And acknowledgment to eldeeem for his color research and granting permission for us to access it. Appreciation also to Tino Di Pietro for his tireless contributions. And a big fat thank you, from the bottom of our hearts, to the staff at the LEGO Store in Cologne – WE LOVE YOU GUYS!

HEEL Verlag GmbH
Gut Pottscheidt
53639 Königswinter
Germany
Tel.: +49 (0) 2223 9230-0
Fax: +49 (0) 2223 9230-13
E-Mail: info@heel-verlag.de
www.heel-verlag.de

© 2015 HEEL Verlag GmbH

Authors: Joachim Klang, Tim Bischoff, Philipp Honvehlmann
Layout, Design and Illustration: Odenthal Illustration, www.odenthal-illustration.de
Photography: Thomas Schultze, www.thomas-schultze.de
Translated from German by: Maisie Fitzpatrick, Susan Ghanouni and Rae Walter in association with First Edition Translations Ltd, Cambridge, UK
Edited by: Kay Hyman in association with First Edition Translations Ltd, Cambridge, UK
Project management: Ulrike Reihn-Hamburger

Printed in Slovakia

ISBN 978-3-95843-134-8

■ CONTENT

■ THE AUTHORS

Tim Bischoff
Although he's the youngest in the group, he's already an old hand.

Joachim Klang
You may know him from other activities, where he goes by the nickname -derjoe-, but it's these colorful bricks that really put a smile on his face.

Philipp Honvehlmann
Also widely known by his nickname, Maydayartist. He's been with us a while, which makes us very happy.

Lutz Uhlmann
The virtual master builder: give him a model and he takes it apart. Once he's done he hands you an instruction manual— and your model back.

Eugen Sellin
Calling him "the plagiator" doesn't go far enough— his developments from our old models are simply phenomenal.

Uwe Kurth
Following decades of LEGO-less existence, Uwe has risen straight to the top. Where can he possibly go from here? Hats off to him.

Jonas Kramm
You may well have heard of "Legopard." He's one of us — welcome to our world.

Christian Treczoks
Behind his back, many people fondly call him "Treebeard." And it's true — he does always give our scenes a lot of greenery.

4

FOREWORD

How did you connect the pieces? Which element have you built in there? What does the model look like from the inside? Which color is that? How did you come up with the idea? We are often asked these and many other questions when we present our models at exhibitions. In this book we have therefore decided to reveal a wide range of construction techniques and demonstrate some of our tips and tricks.
We have not restricted ourselves to listing a series of standalone connections. Instead, we always show them as they appear when built into various models, providing ample inspiration for your own creations, whether houses, cars, spaceships, figures, or even small accessories.

We have also tried to incorporate some exciting themes, with interpretations featuring our models. Approaches include the repurposing of various elements ("nice part usage"), animations ("control the action"), and scenes involving perspective ("forced perspective").

Among our circle the most popular construction elements include rubbers, stickers, flexible tubing (hose rigid 3 mm), levers, minifigure hands, cones, all kinds of clips, and headgear accessories. These components offer myriad possibilities; you will encounter them many times in the following pages.

As LEGO bricks now come in about 130 different colors and shades, we set ourselves the task of using and naming all colors currently being produced at least once within the book. Unfortunately, various platforms such as BrickLink often use color designations that are different from those of LEGO itself. What is commonly known as "dark green" is called "earth green" by LEGO. In turn, LEGO's "dark green" tends to be known simply as "green" elsewhere. Confusing, isn't it? For that reason we have put all of the descriptions alongside one another and their respective colors in an easy-reference table.

As the ultimate colorful construction toy, LEGO offers endless possibilities: you can give your imagination completely free rein. Whether you're using LEGO System, Technic, Duplo, or Clikits, all of the elements can be connected in some way. We have covered every conceivable theme, including cities, science fiction, railways, medieval knights, and cars, at scales ranging from micro and mini to maxi, over the next pages. Prepare to be amazed.

And we have, of course, included some construction guidelines.
So here we go again: it's time to start building!

ABOUT THE BRICKS

How do you source the bricks you need on the internet or from LEGO?

This is a frequent query, but one without a completely straightforward answer. Essentially, there is a distinction between bricks, plates, and tiles. Bricks and plates have studs on the top, while tiles have a smooth upper surface.

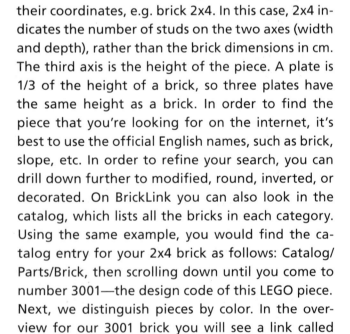

brick   plate   tile

Pieces are defined according to their group and their coordinates, e.g. brick 2x4. In this case, 2x4 indicates the number of studs on the two axes (width and depth), rather than the brick dimensions in cm. The third axis is the height of the piece. A plate is 1/3 of the height of a brick, so three plates have the same height as a brick. In order to find the piece that you're looking for on the internet, it's best to use the official English names, such as brick, slope, etc. In order to refine your search, you can drill down further to modified, round, inverted, or decorated. On BrickLink you can also look in the catalog, which lists all the bricks in each category. Using the same example, you would find the catalog entry for your 2x4 brick as follows: Catalog/Parts/Brick, then scrolling down until you come to number 3001—the design code of this LEGO piece. Next, we distinguish pieces by color. In the overview for our 3001 brick you will see a link called "small images," which leads to a view of all piece codes for this brick. LEGO codes always denote the type of piece and its color, so if our brick were in white, for instance, the code would be 300101.

When this book mentions "BL," it's referring to the BrickLink code, "L-Code" is referring to the LEGO code. Of course, we cannot provide the code for every single one of the pieces featured here, but you will be able to use the method described above to work them out.

LEGO collectors and enthusiasts also talk about Q-parts. These are LEGO bricks that have not appeared in an official set for a certain amount of time, and are unlikely to do so in the foreseeable future. Such rare pieces can, of course, also be found on all kinds of sites or trading platforms. LEGO itself only sells pieces that form part of its current line, which is understandable. So don't despair if you see models that contain unfamiliar pieces or color combinations: you are certain to be able to buy them somewhere. However, as with any area of interest that is popular with collectors, highly sought-after items tend to be rare and/or expensive.

Non-LEGO components and modifications

For many years we have lived by the following motto: "No sticking. No altering pieces. No using non-LEGO components." There are, however, occasions when we have to bend the rules slightly. Narrow, flexible tubing (hose rigid 3 mm) and pneumatic tubing (hose pneumatic 4 mm) are used by the meter at LEGO HQ. You can tell as much by the fact that if you compare several identical tubes from a set with those from another, they are not always exactly the same length. It is common practice among LEGO enthusiasts to shorten these pieces to meet their requirements—indeed, cer tain structural problems may mean that there is no other solution—so we believe that this is justified.

You can also insert one piece of tubing into another. If you cut off pieces to fit, you can actually connect the underside of plates.

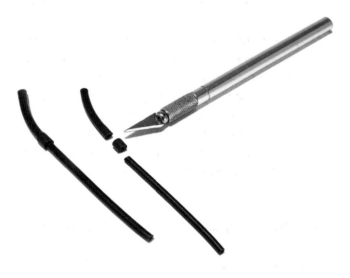

Some of the trains in this book use train wheels made by other manufacturers. And the sails and ropes of the big sailing ship are non-LEGO components. These projects, quite simply, could never have been carried out with original LEGO sails and ropes, or the original train wheels. When you see the results, we hope that you'll forgive us this little lapse. Ultimately, the principle still holds: no non-LEGO parts!

ABBREVIATIONS
Several abbreviations and names circulate in the LEGO fan base:

ABS (Acrylnitril Butadien Styrol)
LEGO bricks are manufactured primarily from this material nowadays

AFOL
Adult Fan of LEGO

MOC
My own creation

TLG (The LEGO Group):
Abbreviation for the company itself

BURP (Big Ugly Rock Piece):
fantastic rocky landscapes can be built with these bricks

LURP (Little Ugly Rock Piece):
the small version

POOP
Pieces that can or should be made of other pieces

LUG (LEGO User Group):
LEGO fan base

TLC (LEGO Train Club):
a LEGO fan base that focuses specifically on building trains

JUMPER
make one out of two: this is a 1x2 plate that has only one stud in the middle.

SNOT (Studs not on top):
this abbreviation refers to a building technique where, using small tricks, for example, an underside can be attached to an underside or the construction direction can be turned 90 degrees. Some examples follow on the next pages.

Cheese Slopes:
sloped bricks–These can be found as 1x1x2/3 and 1x2x2/3 bricks

DEVELOPMENT AND CONSTRUCTION

Before I start to build something, I run through the project in my head. Most of the time, I see something in the street, on TV, or in a video game that I then want to construct out of LEGO. In 2004 I planned to create something large-scale for an exhibition in Berlin (Tausend Steine Land TSL). The shortlist came down to the rocket to the moon from the Tintin comic "Destination Moon," the Post Tower in Bonn or the Empire State Building. As Peter Jackson's remake of "King Kong" was due to come out the following year, I eventually opted for the Empire State Building (ESB). I spent the next few weeks planning which and how many bricks I would need, and working out where I would obtain them. Of course, the most obvious sources were LEGOLAND, the LEGO brand stores, BrickLink, eBay and various flea markets.

Twenty months later—the construction having taken roughly as long as that of the original building—I was finally finished. As the structure was to be formed of bricks stacked into a 3.5 m tower with a weight of approximately 120 kg, and could not therefore be transported in one piece, I built it in 13 modular sections. On the inside I placed all of the secondhand, brightly colored bricks that I could lay my hands upon, for the purposes of stabilization. The outer shell was mainly tan and light gray. For the windows I had ordered around 6000 new trans black 1x2x2 panels (BrickLink no. 4864b), which had to be brand new and free of scratches.

I started with the top of the tower. As a measuring unit I used stacked 8x8 radar dishes (radar dish inverted BL: 2961). I later adapted the ground floor to this module. Meanwhile, I had bought six books about the building, and worked out that in order for my ESB to be to minifigure scale, it had to be about 11 m high. I therefore decided to compress the tower by halving the height of the levels after the first building stage. As the tower looked accurate when appraised by eye, I decided to finish it at a height of 3.5 m.

Despite its size, various construction techniques were used for the Empire State Building; I'd like to mention them here. For instance, the green lead glazing over the main entrance consists of countless little transparent and black plates, with a second layer of green bricks. The whole window was then rotated 90° and inserted horizontally.

As the building was to be displayed free-standing, I created a rear façade with a loading ramp and back entrance. The roller doors consist of horizontally laid flexible tubing (hose rigid 3 mm), which allowed me to determine the size of the door opening myself. Two archways are built around the ventilation opening, the lower of which was rotated 180° and then fitted. My model of the Empire State Building is now over 10 years old, but I've never had the heart to demolish it.

Another example is the way in which I built my police car. The 1992 LAPD Ford Crown Victoria had long been on my wish list. I had noticed it in various films, and when I saw a real one I was convinced that the time had come to make the model. Most models undergo a gradual building process, so I was already pretty pleased with my first version of the Ford.

After long consideration, however, the C-pillar did not look round enough, so I began a second attempt, in which I gave the roof edge curved elements and replaced the molding of the trunk. At the same time, the fittings inside the car were altered to make it more stable. The searchlights on the hood are operated from inside the driver's cab, so I left off the lever. I then spent another day looking at the car closely, with the result that I decided to rebuild it again.

In the third and final version, the hood had to be partially shifted forward. I also inserted two headlight bricks at an angle in order to achieve a gap of half a stud.

I replaced the lever base with a 1x1 round plate. I used a 2x2 hinge brick (top plate thin, BL 6134) to lift the signal lights a little. And in order to prevent the 1x2 tiles, which serve here as door handles, from sliding inward, they are blocked from the inside.

There are four versions of the 1x1 modified plates with clip:

 • **Thick U-ring**

 • **Thin U-ring**

 • **Thick O-ring**

 • **Thin O-ring**

It is better to use the thicker versions for the car's rear-view mirror holder, as the clamped tiles are less likely to fall out.
However, if the clips are used to ensure a smooth surface, as they are here, you should use the thin versions—the thick ones won't fit.

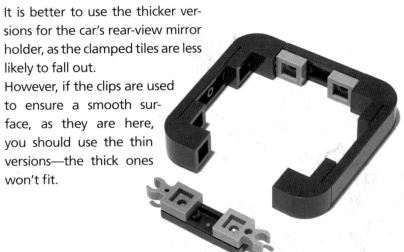

◼ REPURPOSING PIECES

We have already mentioned some abbreviations used in LEGO jargon. In this chapter we intend to look at NPU (Nice Part Usage) more closely—in other words, the repurposing of pieces. The above example shows two saddles with printed tiles as eyes, which transforms them into two heads having a conversation. It's a little abstract, but very effective.

With this Bernese mountain dog I wanted to show that you can make wonderful constructions with very ordinary bricks. Leaving special bricks aside and simply building brick upon brick, you can make recognizable and lifelike models. I only paid attention to the choice of colors.

I only allowed myself to play around a little when creating the tongue, which is a loosely inserted orange brick separator.

When working on "my own creations," or MOCs, you can also insert elements that were not necessarily intended as bricks, such as the packaging for the X-Pod range, which Phil used as a key element in his TV Tower.

Another good example is the protective frames in which the leaves (plant flower stem 1 x 1 x 2/3 with 3 large leaves, BL: x8) are embedded when new. When they are first used, they are pulled out at predetermined breaking points, but they can also work well when used as tendrils, for instance, and built into the project. We will demonstrate this in greater detail in the chapter on plants.

The weather vane of the mountain castle provides a further illustration of NPU: You can use hammers for the four points of the compass. The thin pin for the feathers of the cockerel (BL: 64647) fits into a small hole on the bar with clip (BL: 48729b). The beak is a minifigure hand.

These and many other NPUs can be found throughout the book—simply look at all of the pictures closely, and you will spot them.

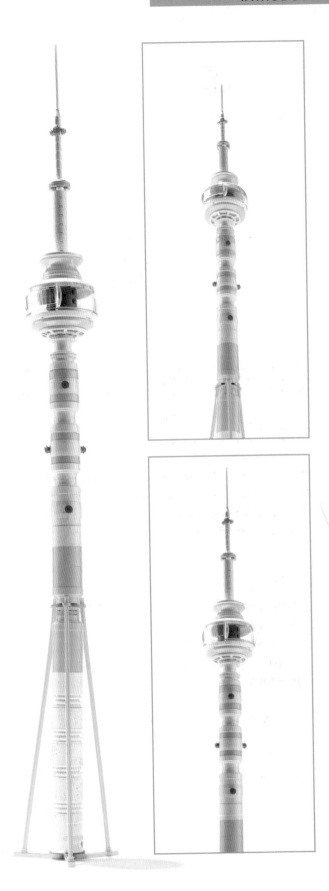

CONTROL THE ACTION

This is what we call images or models that give the impression that they are capturing an action shot. Ultimately, however, the vital thing is to create a stable model. One example is the explosion of a tan limousine in a car park overrun by zombies, in which the flames seem to flicker and the figure appears to be flying through the air.

The following short series of images shows the way in which an action scene develops over several images—after all, there are few better examples of rapid, spontaneous change than in an explosion. The shed (with explosive contents) has a concrete roof and pillars. The space between these pillars consists of boarded walls with a window and doors. As in real life, the images show that pressure always takes the path of least resistance, so the window, walls, and door are the first victims. I was inspired to create this whole scene by a slow-motion video on YouTube, in which exactly this kind of building was blown up.

In the first picture (on page 18), everything is as it should be. Only the sign on the corner of the building suggests that there might be something volatile in the bushes or inside the shed...

In the second picture we see the immediate effect of the detonation inside the shed. This is accompanied by the first flash of flames, as could also be seen in the video. The tiles were all fixed to clips and could thus be positioned at just about any angle required. The fire inside is simulated by four LEGO light bricks (electric, light brick 2 x 3 x 1 1/3 with trans-clear top and yellow LED light (glows orange) BL + LEGO: 54930c02), three of them glowing yellow and one red. In order for the light to look right, it requires a kind of "canvas," which is achieved by placing transparent bricks as a wall behind the outer boarded wall.

In the third picture the boards are no longer joined together. The glass is broken in two, the door has been torn from its hinges, and the window shutters have been blasted out. The initial fire has gone out, and everything that was loose or unfixed has been forced out of the shed. In the video that served as a model, large amounts of dust and smoke streamed out of all the holes that had been blown in the former wall. This has been represented here with the use of flexible tubing in gray and black, the lengths depicting the straight-up trajectory of the particles. The wooden panels are now fixed to long clip rods, or—as in the case of the uppermost one—to a long antenna, the round head of which is inserted into a clip, once again with a tile pressed into it. Many kinds of transparent rod elements can be used to represent these sorts of loose positions, but I have only used a few here for reasons of space.

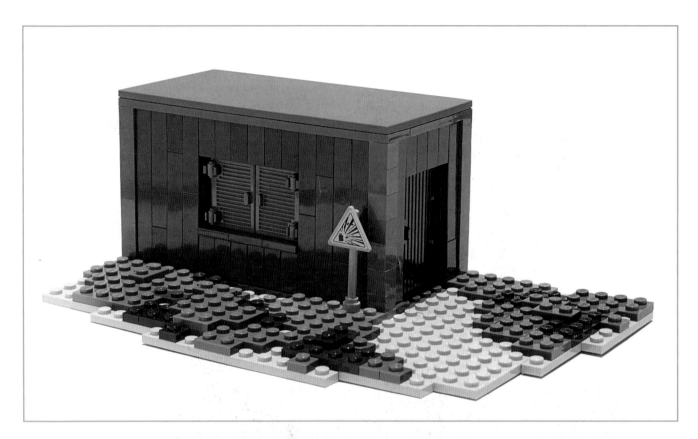

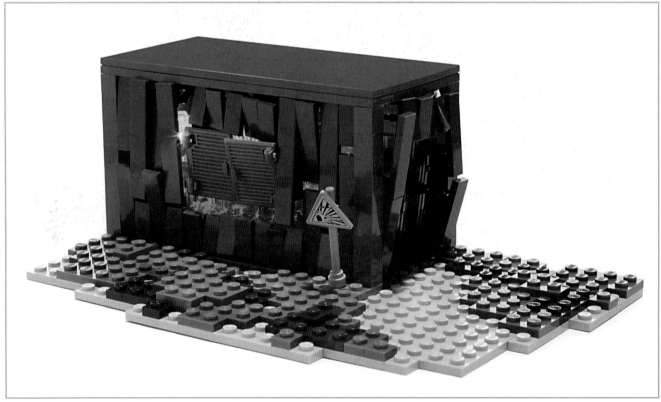

FORCED PERSPECTIVE

This term covers images in which the observer obtains a particular impression by viewing the model from a certain perspective, as opposed to seeing the scene as it really is. As such, the photo on page 23 reproduces the famous endless staircase of Maurits Escher. In the view from above, the illusion is perfect. However, the left-hand photos show the greater length of the lower end and the significant difference in height from the top of the stairs.

The intentional use of blurring can also help to deceive the eye into taking on board the intended impression. In the old but classic famous scene from "Monty Python and the Holy Grail," which has achieved cult status, we show that ostensibly large objects don't actually have to be built on a large scale if you use this trick. Castle Camelot in the background is barely bigger than the figures in the foreground. The flat perspective and the blurring of the background allow us to simulate distance, which our brains interpret as a difference in size, due to experience. However, you have to strike a precise balance between the perspective and the level of blurring. If the background is too sharp, the viewer will see the true proportions, while, if it is too blurred, the viewer will no longer be able to recognize what the object is. In comparison with the large photo, you can see that a completely focused image cannot achieve the right effect. The actual composition of the scene is only evident from a bird's eye view, which reveals the true distances and elements involved.

For this scene we have once again conjured up some rare pieces: the coconut shells that Patsy is holding in his hands are brown lever bases. For the King, we used the new Snowtrooper outfit, and his crown is from the Collectable Minifigures series.

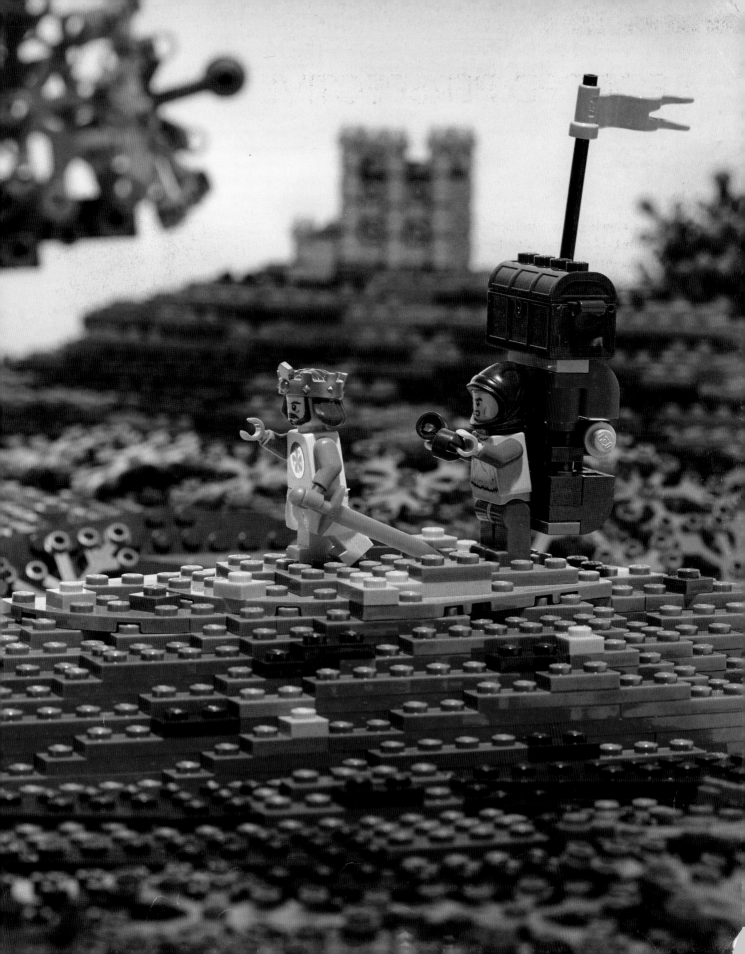

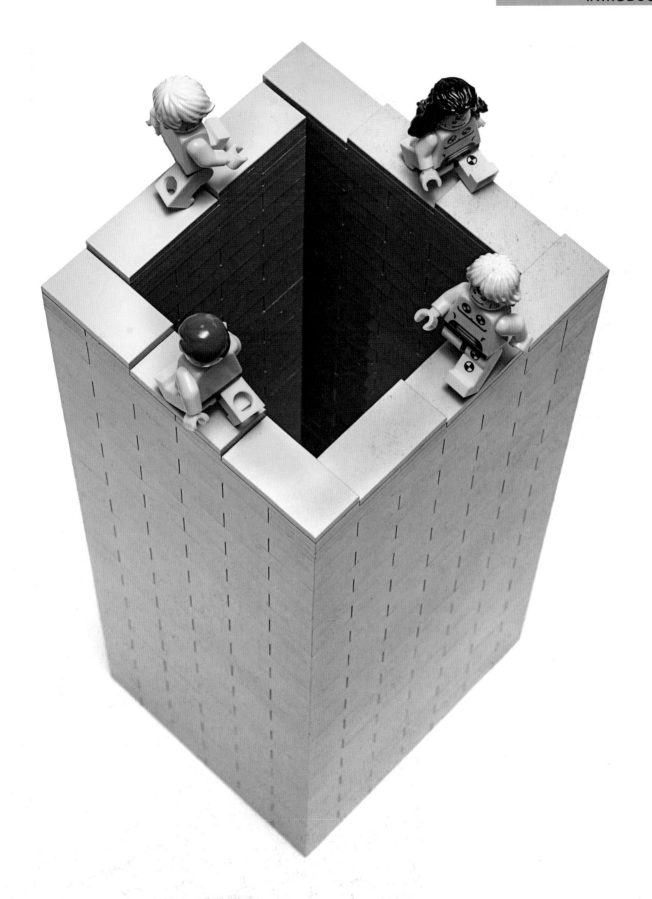

SNOT

SNOT (studs not on top) means—as suggested—a construction technique that makes it possible to build "around corners," as it were, thus changing the building direction within a model.

Almost all of our models were built using this process to some degree. There are countless ways of diverting the building direction, which we illustrate throughout this book. Here, we wish to demonstrate the technique using the example of a cube. All of this cube's surfaces are faced with tan tiles (tile, modified 2x2 inverted, BL: 11203). This is possible if you use a simple trick: by placing two panel walls back to back, you get the right width to jam them between two studs. Look closely at the photo showing the inside of the cube, and you will see how it is all being held together.

The upper example could be properly "snotted," and could serve as the awning for a shop window, for instance.

Another important SNOT element is the old hinge plate (hinge plate 2x5 BL: 3149c01 or 2x9 BL: 3324c01). These were used between 1967 and 2003

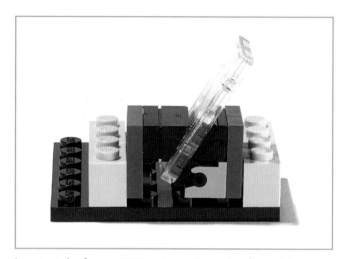

in a total of over 250 sets and can be found in most older LEGO collections. Using a small Technic axle, you can push in the small splint that you need to join the undersides of two bricks together (see page 26).

THE MINIONS

Few phenomena have captured the collective imagination in recent years like these chaos-causing buffoons. Countless minions have also been created in LEGO. I mulled over an idea for building one for a long time before I actually carried it out. The SNOT technique comes into its own in my model, where a hinge plate is used to connect the undersides of two bricks. This is the only way to join curves upwards and downwards in such a small space. By making a few structural changes, the arms can also go in different directions. In addition, the missile trajectory provides another example of a "control the action" scene. Banana?

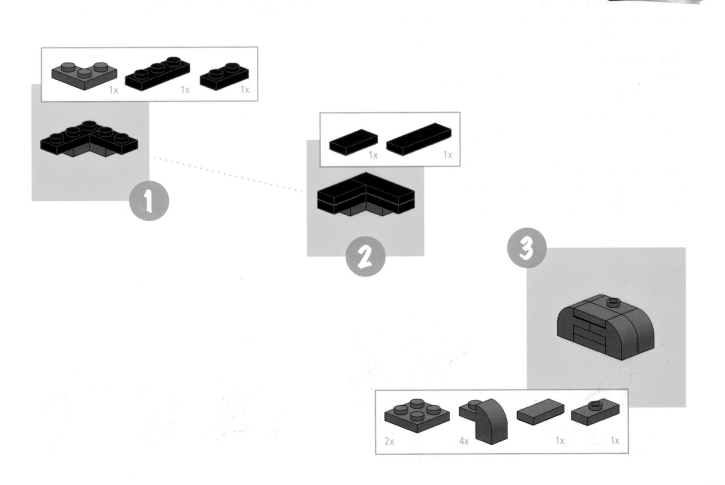

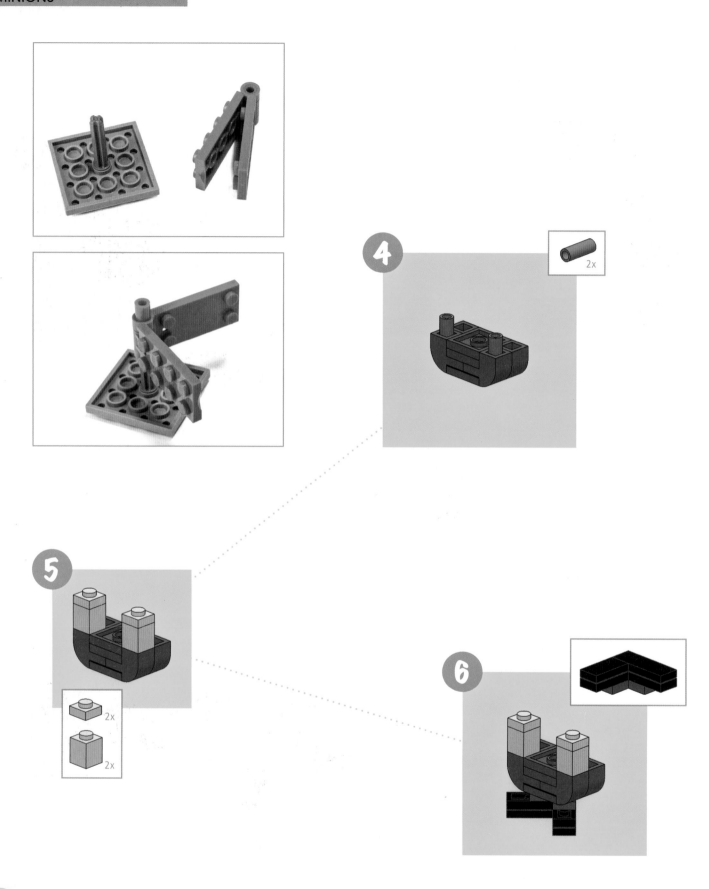

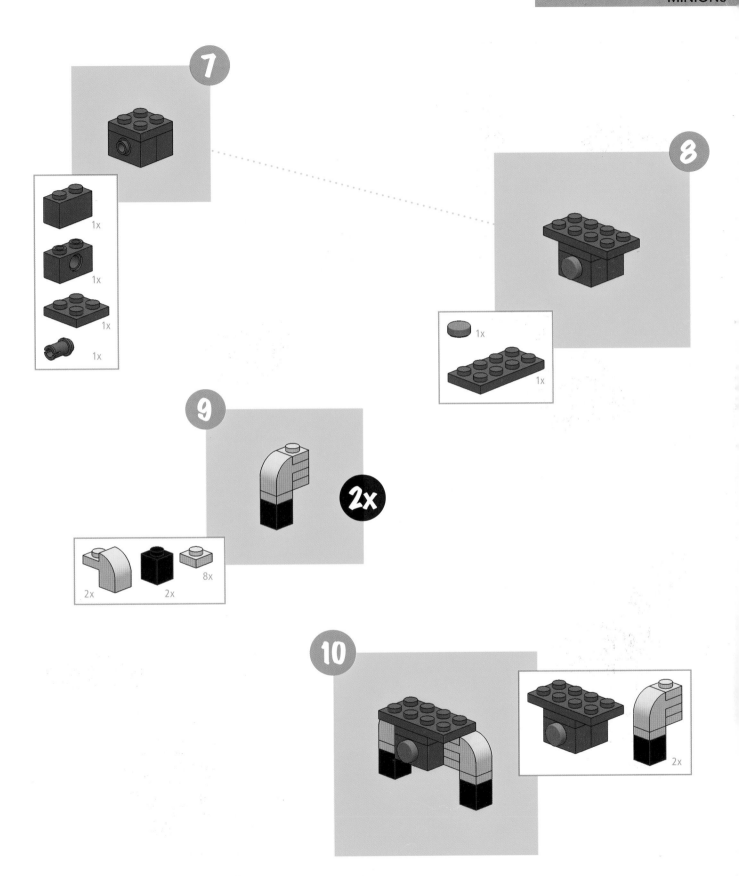

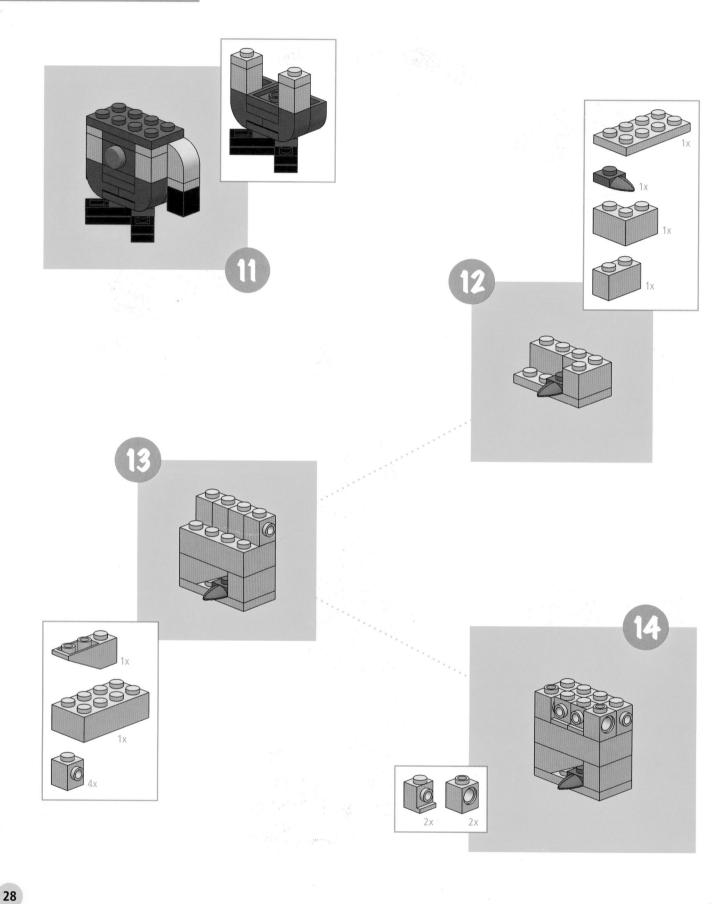

15

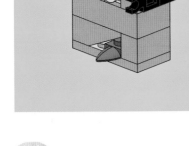

16

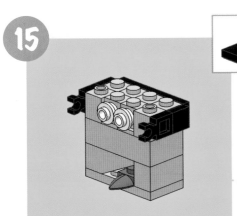

This is not a bar 3L, but a cut reddish brown Technic Flex-System hose. Alternatively you can use a flexo or omit the pupils.

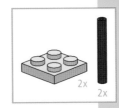

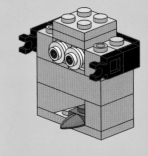

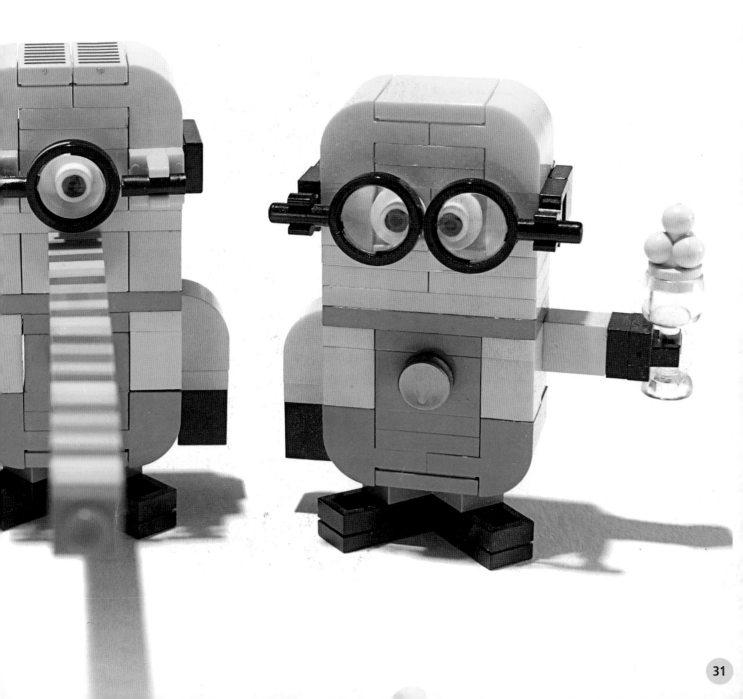

17

18

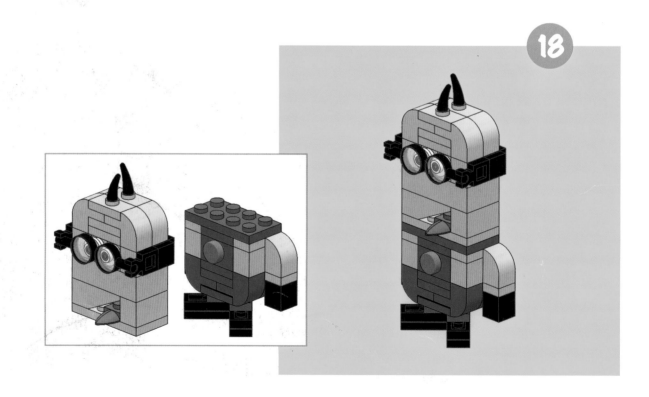

PARTS LIST

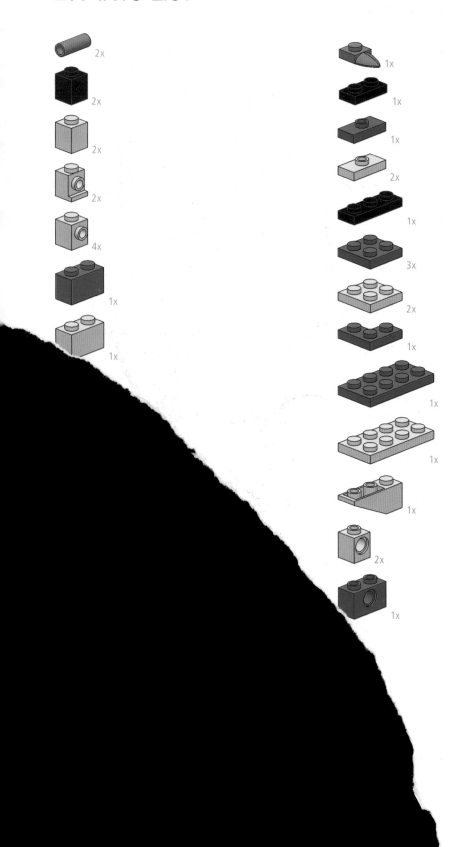

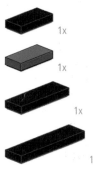

Quantity	Color		Element	Element Name
2		Red	313	Hinge Plate 2 x 5
2		Black	3005	Brick 1 x 1
2		Yellow	3005	Brick 1 x 1
2		Yellow	4070	Brick 1 x
4		Yellow	87087	Brick
1		Blue	3004	B
1		Yellow	3004	
4		Blue	6091	
6		Yellow	6091	
1		Yellow	2357	
1		Yellow	3001	
2		Black	53451	
2		Black	10830	
10		Yellow	3024	
2		White	858	
2		Black	40	
1		Red		
1		Black		
1		Blue		
2		Yellow		
1		Black		
3		Blue		
2		Yellow		
1		Blue		
1		Blue		
1		Yellow		
1		Yellow		
2		Yellow		
1		Blue		
2		Reddish Brow		
1		Blue		
1		Flat Silver		
2		Black		
1		Black		
1		Blue		
1		Black		
1		Black		

RNITURE

iar with those images of perfectly
ooms, bedrooms, or dining rooms
ogs and advertising brochures,
oks immaculate and the rooms
less space. Partitioned spaces in
en specially installed furnish-
often serve as the settings
tside the frame of the pic-
and empty. This can also
perspective—as in the case
rooms are arranged
from which photos
from above,
ld reveal

ut

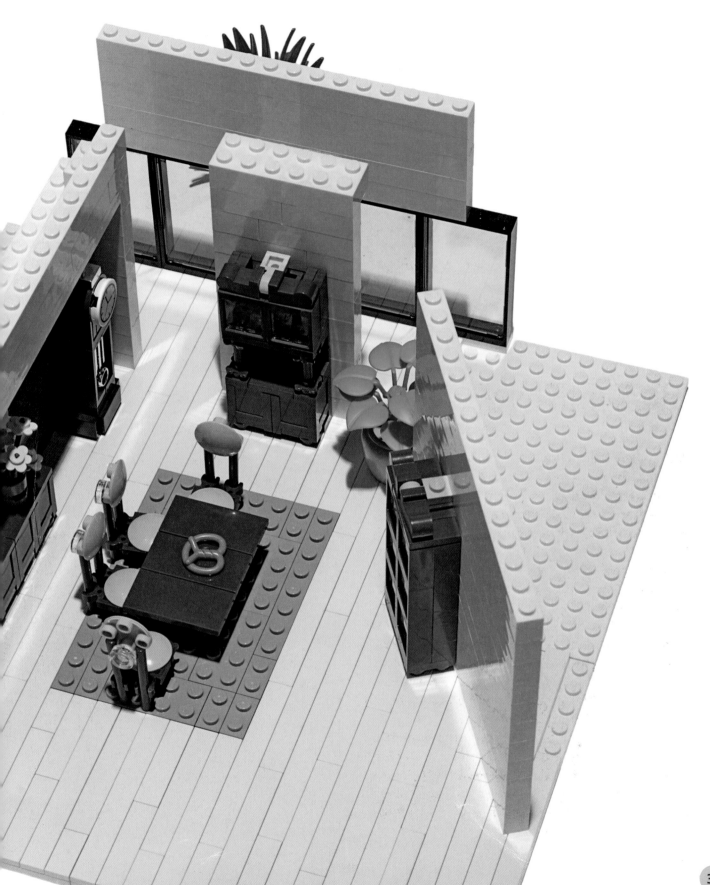

SIDEBOARD AND GRANDFATHER CLOCK

When making pieces of furniture, I tend to come back to the brown box (container, box 2x2x2 – top opening BL + LEGO: 61780). By simply giving it a plate or tile as a lid, or—even better—by stacking it, the ornament on the outside of the box comes to resemble the carvings on a cabinet door. The dresser is thus made up of several clamped-together boxes, connected to a 1x8 plate at the lower rear edge. The vase of flowers on the sideboard is a rubberless tire rim. (There are only seven sets that contain this piece in that shade.)

The grandfather clock uses a clamping technique for the pendulum and the clock-face. You can see the individual pieces clearly in the adjacent photo. Essentially, they are inserted between two panels at the bottom, and into a castle window, with its grille removed, at the top. A brown 1x1 brick can also be built in to form the base of the clock-face. I opted to use two plates and a 1x1 tile rotated 180°, as the 1x2 tile has a small groove that is repeated in the 1x1 tile. These days you would have to find a new piece for the clock-face, as LEGO has changed the rear side of it. Previously, it had a cross in the middle, which pressed between the studs. Today the usual round-holed stud is used on the underside, allowing the clock-face to be fastened easily to the stud of the headlight brick.

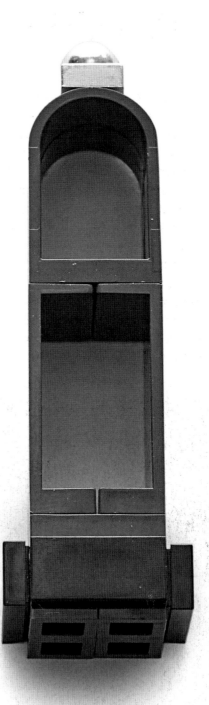

WELSH DRESSER

The Welsh dresser is an eye-catching piece, with a number of special design features. I started at the bottom with two of the aforementioned boxes, and then placed a long, brown panel in length 4 and two mini flower pieces (plate, round 1x1 with flower edge, four studs, BL + LEGO: 33291) on top of these, along with a few normal building components. The mini flower pieces are very important, as they can be used together with two pieces of flexible tubing cut to length to form the connection between the upper and lower parts of the dresser. Two windows are then fixed to the front of the upper part, and at the very top the wreath is fixed to the back wall using a mini flower. The holed stud of the mini flower is the key detail here. The wreath itself consists of minifigure legs. If you wish, you could start with the inside and build outwards, in which case you could see the hole with which the leg is attached to the hip joint.

CHAIRS

As fans, we are always curious about what new pieces are coming out of the LEGO workshop, and we try to build them into the models that we are working on. One such piece is the transparent tile with a holed pin (trans-clear tile, round 1x1 with pin, BL + LEGO: 20482). When used in our dining room chairs, these allow the backrest to be clamped to the long chair legs. The other elements of the chair are as follows: two boat glides, two sections of shortened flexible tubing, two vertical clips, and two mini flower pieces.

PIANO AND CABINET

There are countless ways of making a piano, especially when it comes to the keys. I wanted to build the keyboard using gear shift levers, and found that a single gear shift lever fits beautifully between two studs when their undersides are fastened to a studded base. Of course, there is no need to represent all of the keys, as long as it is easy to see what is intended.

The glass-doored cabinet matches the upper part of the dresser. In this case, it was necessary to rotate the back wall 180° in order for the tan O-ring clip to be fastened to the top.

LIVING ROOM

We probably don't need to say a great deal about the seating in the next image. The 6x8 plate in white, used as a shag rug, almost counts as NPU. The floor lamp is also built from only a few pieces. Standard plates form the pedestal and the lampshade at the top and bottom. The shade of the reading lamp is actually a fez (Ottoman-style hat).

ROCKING CHAIR AND PLASTIC CHAIR

Furniture at minifigure scale is very small, and if you want to replicate details you will have to delve into your box of tricks. The spiral sides of this rocking chair are made from a circular whip. The feet of the white plastic chair are made of small horns that were inserted into holed studs at an angle.

OFFICE FURNITURE

The roller frame of the executive chair consists of the grey rotating pieces of a turntable, which can be separated from their using a pin or rod. A 1x1 round plate with a hole is fastened to the now freestanding middle pin, which is then placed under one of the new negative tiles, along with four backpack holders, between the four studs. Two of the backpack holders point backwards, while the other two point left and right. The backrest is made of two 1x3 tiles and a boat glide. However, the highlights are the armrests: these consist of a pair of binoculars and a revolver, and are clipped into the backpack holders. For the color we stuck to dark gray, the only shade in which all of the parts were available.

One piece, which makes regular appearances in this book, is the relatively new cone (cone 1 1/6 x 1 1/6 x 2/3 (Fez) BL: 85975). In the next image it is used as a cup in medium blue, connected to the Thermos flask with a Technic half pin (BL: 4274). The desk lamp also uses the element, this time in dark red. A tile (round 2x2 tile with hole, BL: 15535) and a round plate (1x1 with open stud, BL: 85861) are used for the pedestal. These pieces have only been on the market since 2013 and 2009 respectively, and are not particularly well known.

And, finally, a whole cluster of ideas: if you stack several cones together, you can make a neat yucca plant trunk, and if you put flowers in a cone, you get a flowerpot like the one on the shelf of the Swedish furniture store shown here. The saucer for this almost dehydrated plant is a simple radar dish, placed in a 1x2 Technic brick (BL: 3700), so that the stud disappears. I imitated Uwe's models for all of the carriages and the little locomotive—we will see the originals later in the book. The wheels of the little railway engines are minifigure roller skates (BL: 11253, LEGO: 6088585). The drinking bird (also known as a perpetual mobile device of the second kind) essentially consists of a maraca (BL: 90301pb01) pushed firmly into a bucket (BL: 95343). The fruit bowl is the porthole of a panel (BL: 30080), which—if it has not been ultrasonically welded—can be pulled out. Hinges (BL: 2429c01) are used as drawers for the desk. Oh yes, and the door of the freight car is a headlight (BL: 4070) laid flat.

1958 PLYMOUTH FURY – CHRISTINE

We were catching up at our regular LEGO meet, and I had brought along a few cars. Uwe asked me whether I had ever built Christine, the car from Stephen King's book of the same name. My ears pricked up. Some of our friends believed this car to be a Cadillac, but one look on the internet revealed the truth: Christine is a 1958 Plymouth Fury. Its many rounded edges suggested that creating a replica of it would be a difficult task, but I actually managed to plan the model within two days. In the photo on page 58 you can see that I used a method of simply stacking various snotted structures. Joining the windscreen and roof together presented the biggest challenge, but fortunately there is a 1x1 modified plate with a thick ring that is different from the current version, produced between 1980 and 2006 (plate, modified 1x1 with clip light

– thin ring, BL: 4081a). This allowed me to redirect the studs within the narrow space. The image of the underside of the car shows how the upper elements are held together by the undercarriage.

Matching tires are always hard to find once you exceed a certain size, despite LEGO being the world's biggest tire manufacturer. In this case I used the trick of inserting one tire into another. By turning the outer tire left and kneading it in your hand a little, it warms up and becomes softer, allowing it to be slipped over another tire with ease. In particularly stubborn cases or if the outer tire needs to be thicker, you could even stretch it over a cone.

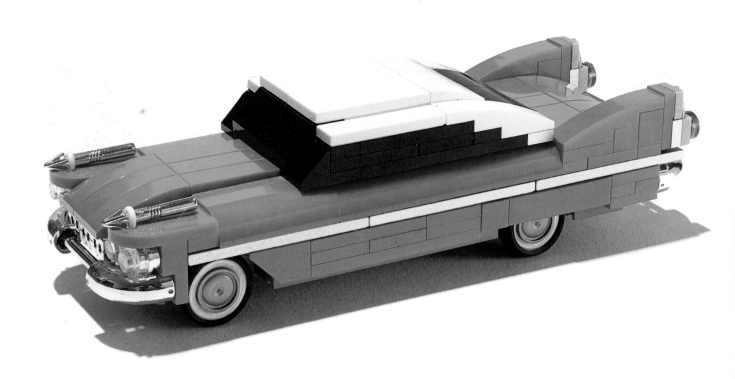

In order to make the radiator grill stable, I used the old gear shift lever trick (see photo). The fenders could be given a smooth look only by using Q-parts and rubber rings. Luckily, on BrickLink I found the modified tiles (modified 3x2 with hole, BL: 48995) that I needed in red. To be on the safe side, I also ordered them in white. This was a wise decision, as will later be revealed. The silver rod (bar 4.5L with stop ends, BL: 71184) fits perfectly in the middle of the bumper.

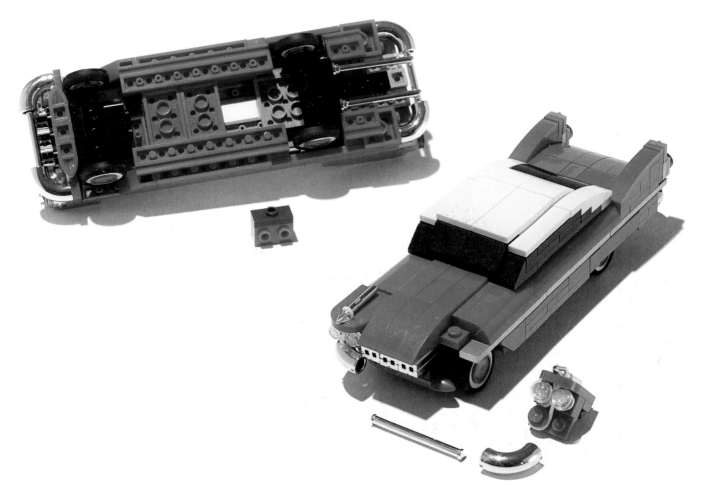

As I was waiting for the pieces to be delivered, I made a quick, run-down version of the old-timer: rusty and dented, with a dull coat of paint, missing fuel cap, and moss and a green patina on the windows, and so on. The bumpers are once again made of Q-parts (round brick 1x1 90° elbow—no stud, BL: 71075)—I once bought these in old grey on a trading platform. We purposely did not wipe away the dust that had settled on the car when we came to take this photo. The ordered parts finally arrived, and I was able to continue.

And because I liked the model so much, I tried it in a different color. I christened this one Peppermint Patty.

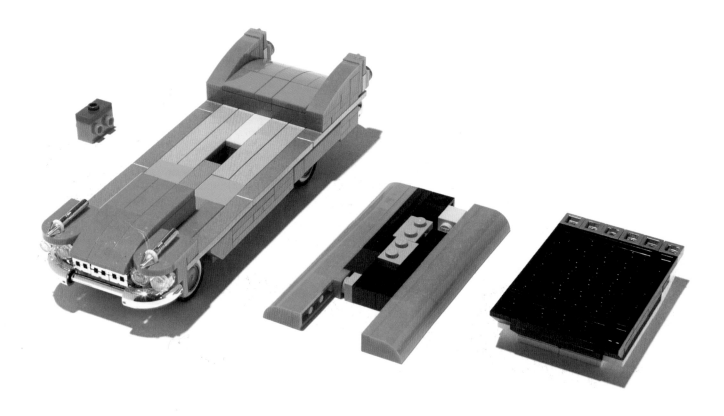

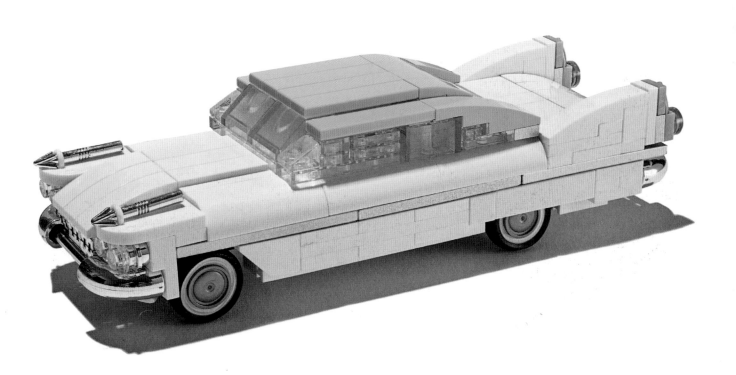

VW TYPE 2 T2 „BULLI"

Once LEGO issued a set for the T1, I thought that the "Bulli" was done and dusted. But then I thought, hey, there's nothing at minifigure size, so I attempted the T2. This resulted in a number of very different versions. I identified various approaches, and built corresponding models in different colors. The core feature was the central part, with finger joints (hinge plate 1x2 with 2 fingers BL: 4276 and 3 fingers 4275) used to change the building direction.

In the photo of the disassembled police Bulli it is easy to make out how the individual modules look in the final version. The Technic brick with pin was used at the front end out of necessity, as all of my 1x1 bricks with side studs were being used in other models at that point in time. This alternative nicely demonstrates a possible option, should one of the pieces you need be missing. The police Bulli also shows how you can use carefully chosen stickers to create lively details.

I used a hammer (BL: 6246b) as the closure buckle for the municipal garbage truck. A bit of SNOT was also used to create a smooth plane.

Some day I will add bits of AC/DC stickers on the side of the black Bulli with shuttered windows from the film "Maximum Overdrive," as I think this will add to the effect.

This example has another interesting feature—the two types of gear shift. The smaller and older version can be pushed into clips or the hands of figures. For this reason they are often used as car antennae or—as in this case—windshield wipers.

And sometimes you just have to strike it lucky—during the building process exactly the piece I needed to give the lime green/white model additional headlights on its bumpers (tile, round 1x1 with pin, BL: 20482, LEGO: 6112751) came onto the market.

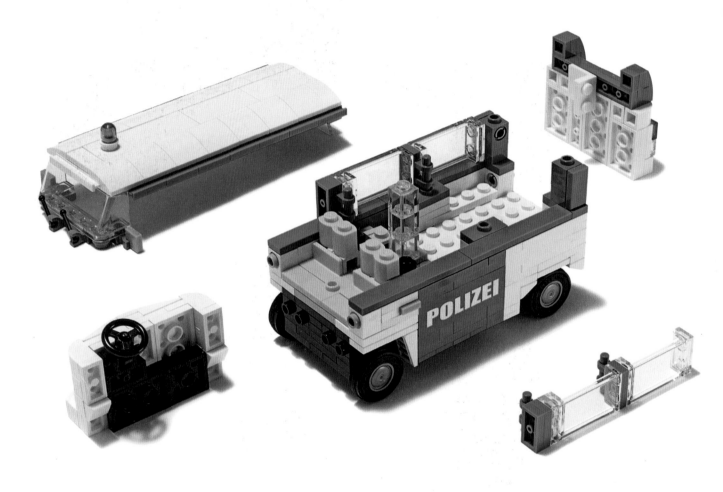

BABY STROLLER AND SHOPPING CART

Since these small models also feature in the picture, we have included an exploded-view photo to show how they are made.

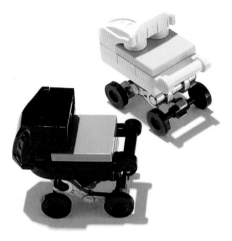
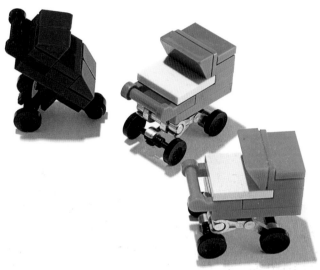

1976 CHEVROLET CORVETTE C3 COUPÉ

I saw one of these cars driving around my home town a few weeks ago, and that very same evening I built it in white. In order to simulate the many rounded edges on the lower part of the car, I had to resort to a trick: you can use finger joints to scale a 7W (width) effectively down to 6W. 7W is an abbreviation for 7 wide, and refers to the number of studs. In order to make models to the correct scale for minifigures, some builders use a width of 6W. However, old-fashioned American cars and even some new models with the latest hubcaps (from the Speed Champions collection) require something approaching the 7W size.

Let's linger over this design icon a little longer. It would make a great getaway car for a gang of bank robbers, wouldn't it?

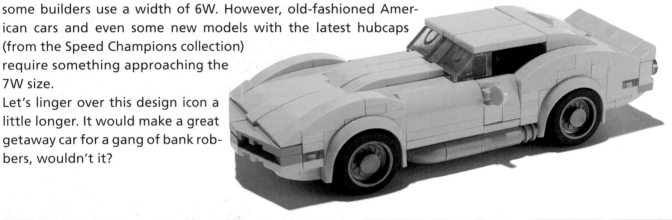

BANK ROBBERY

As the bank building itself is so striking, we wanted to include it in the scene. The street in front of the bank is actually a wall on its side, allowing the narrow road markings to be laid out effectively. It's up to you whether you want to make the roadway black or dark gray. We show the different effects in the photos below.

At the entrance to the bank the tiles are stacked on a single stud, so that they can be adjusted as required. The window beside the door uses the old hinge plate trick.

SWAT TRUCK

Even when the bank robbery scene was still at the idea stage, we were sure that we wanted to show a special task force in addition to the normal police cars and officers, with a matching SUV. The model centers around the police SUV, which can be seen at the edge of the activity. As in real life, the SWAT team does not sit in the vehicle, but clings to the outside, so that they can swing into action as soon as they arrive at the scene, without having to waste time clambering out.

OUTSIDE BROADCASTING VEHICLE

When there's a bank robbery, it's never long before the local media arrive. As in our model, outside broadcasting vehicles often get there before the SWAT team, to report and speculate on the crime.

Of course, a bank heist scene is not complete without the press and a rapid response team. Their weapons have been constructed using tools such as binoculars, hammers, tubing, and hands. Small lengths of tubing are difficult to stretch over hands. As an aid or quick fix, simply place a bar in a minifigure's hand.

2007 FORD SHELBY GT 500 SVT

This Ford Shelby GT 500 SVT is based on another film: "I Am Legend." Since I had already created an iconic New York landmark in the form of the Empire State Building, part of the set for the photo was already to hand. I suddenly realized in the midst of photo shooting for this book that I had no deer figures so I quickly created some overnight, perhaps with not the most sophisticated of results but I did not want to end up simply copying something. The new 1x2 curved slope pieces (slope, curved 2x1 no studs BL: and LEGO: 11477) were a real help in constructing these animals. The signal paddles (minifig, utensil signal paddle BL: 3900) in brown are also known as Q-parts but are available from BrickLink at an average cost of approx. US$0.57. As you can see, I used a mixture of brown and reddish brown, which helped in creating coat markings.

This car is also a very good example of how used sticker sheets can be put to good use. Once all the stickers on a LEGO sticker sheet have been utilized, there are often strips of color left over around the pressed-out sticker. This is particularly useful when it occurs between two sticker motifs of the same color, and is how I achieved the narrow red stripe that runs right down the center of the car. As with the Corvette, I constructed the new mudguards (vehicle, mudguard 4 x 2 1/2 x 2 1/3 with arch, round, BL: 18974) and tires by utilizing parts from the new Speed Champions series. The chassis is likewise constructed in 7W, with the driver's cab narrowing to 6W. I shaped around the front corners using the same technique as with my VW bus.

For comparison purposes, I am including a photo of an older Mustang model, which I created some time ago and which does not have the latest mudguards. It, too, was constructed using the 7W/6W combination.

The tires—as is often the case—are made from two rubber bands, stretched one over the other. Another rubber band was also stretched around the front to simulate the curved design.

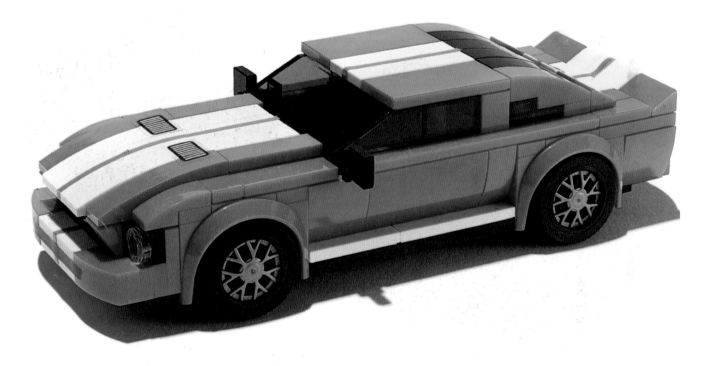

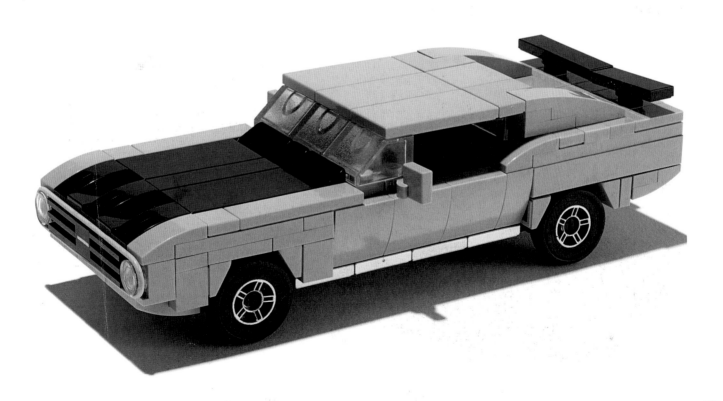

■SUV

Speed Champion tires can also be used for 6W cars, as demonstrated by this SUV. The vehicle combines several of the techniques mentioned earlier, such as curving around the front corners, the 1x2 tiles inserted to form door handles, and the old, smaller gearshift used as an antenna. It goes without saying that you could also use the larger gearshift with the base. Something that may not be immediately noticeable is that the rear axle is one tile higher, which lends the vehicle a sportier appearance. The radiator is made from two curved pieces (slope, curved 2x2 no studs, 3 side ports recessed, BL: 44675). The roof rails are made from rods and the windscreen wipers consist of levers pushed into place.

1976 TRIUMPH BONNEVILLE

We were inspired to reproduce this motorcycle by the popular TV series "The Walking Dead." Building a motorcycle on a minifigure scale presents a particular challenge: it is difficult to construct something as intricate as this in recognizable form. A model of this type consists of many tiny elements and, as the photo shows, is held together in numerous places by clips. Some of the hoses also have to be shortened to the correct length. The chrome bar is a bucket handle (BL: 71861) from the Belville series. The wheel rims have been taken from bicycles, then fitted with car tires turned inside out. For a clearer overview, we have included a photo showing the underside of the motorcycle.

Daryl Dixon's crossbow could only be created with a piece of hose, which I used to make one of the binocular lens openings narrower so that the end of the crossbow arrow would fit snugly into it (minifig, weapon compound bow with arrow, BL: 10258 and LEGO 6004944).

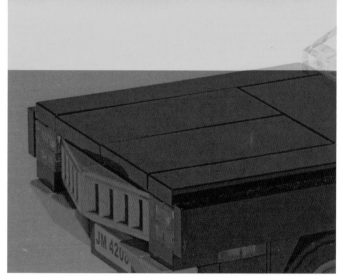

With only a few modifications you can build all these models by following the building instructions on the next pages

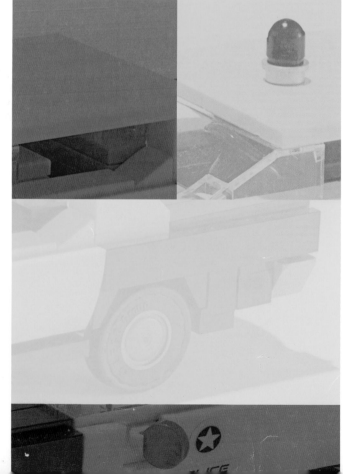

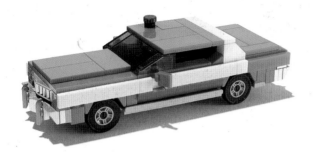

1969 PLYMOUTH BELVEDERE

When I began working on the Ford Crown Victoria, I looked up a large number of cars on the internet using the search terms Police Car black white. In doing so, I stumbled across this Old-timer and knew as soon as I saw it that I wanted to build this Plymouth as well. This time, however, I devised a method of construction completely different from my usual procedure. The trick in this case was to design a car that could be transformed in just a few steps into a different vehicle—in other words, one based on a universal frame. Even just changing the color is enough to turn it into a civilian car. But if the fenders are modified or different elements are used for the side paneling, it is possible to create a totally new model. If you want to lengthen the C-pillar or trunk, it is very simple to extend the car at the rear by incorporating an additional plate with studs on the sides (plate, modified 2 x 2 x 2/3 with 2 studs on side, BL: 99206 and LEGO: 4654577)—as shown on the photo on page 104. The following pages contain complete instructions for building this old police car.

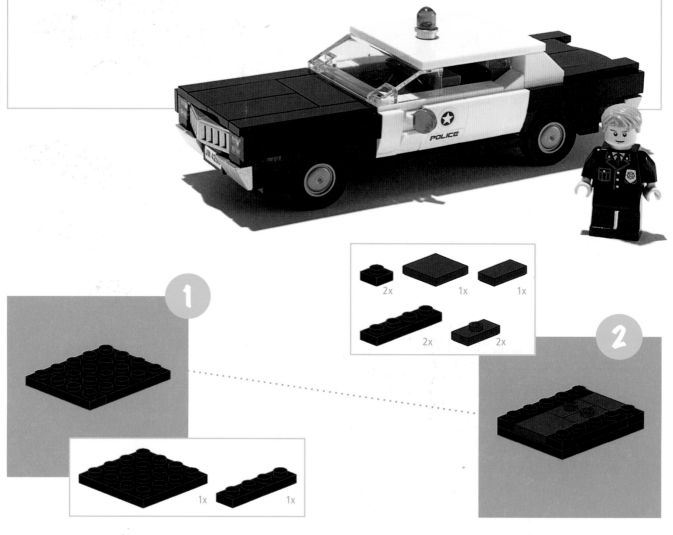

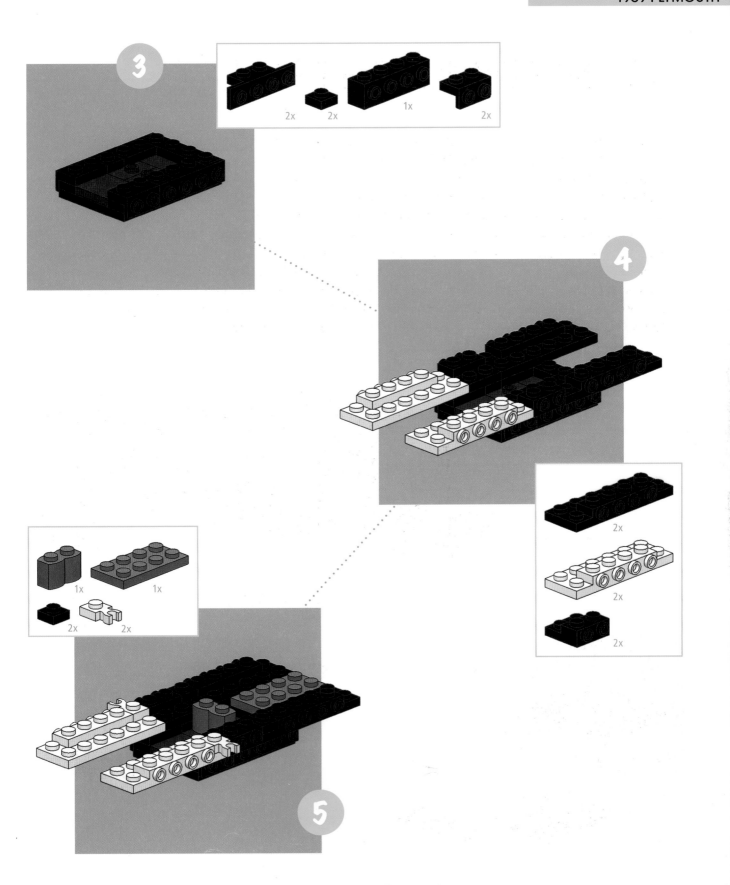

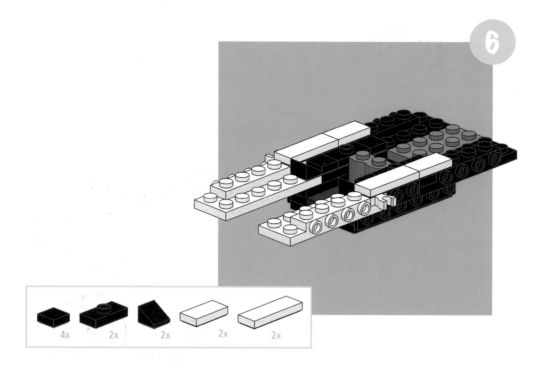

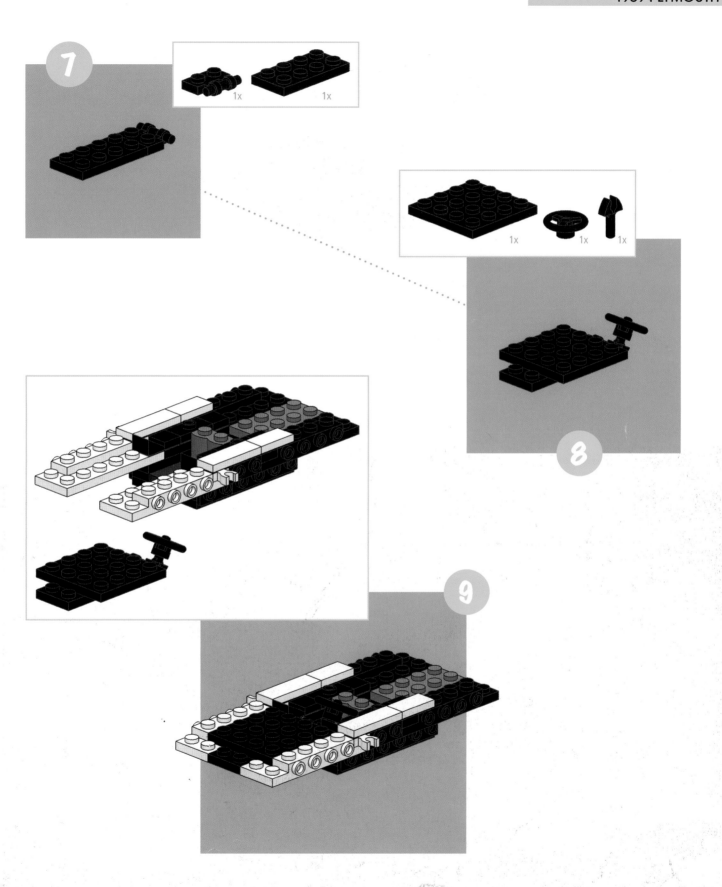

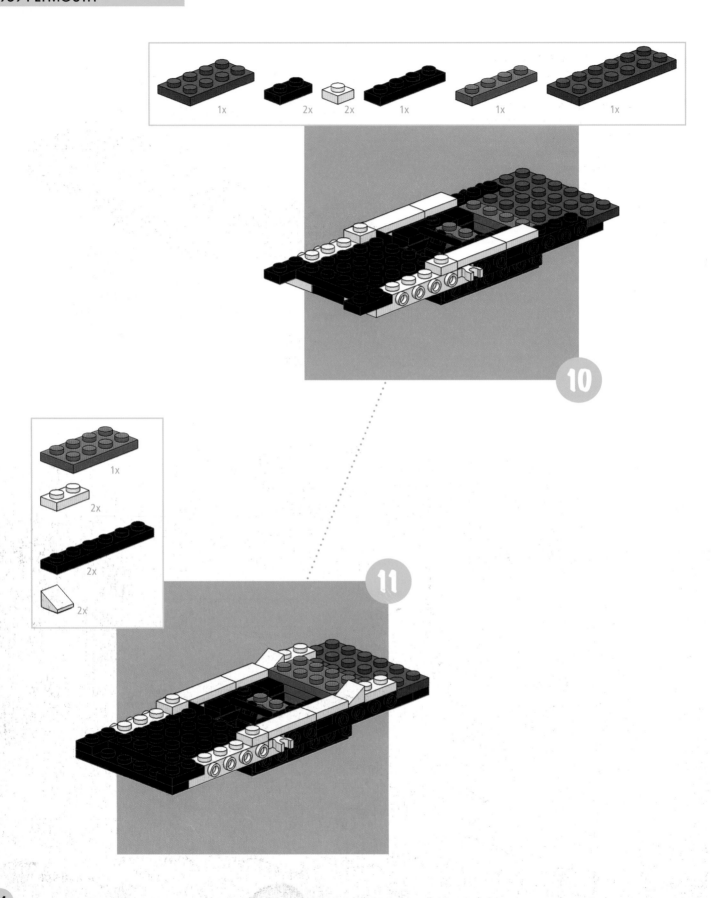

The trunk lid can later be moved one row further back. In this case, it is advisable to fix a 1x4 plate under the rear window. But finish constructing the model first: you can decide later which option you prefer.

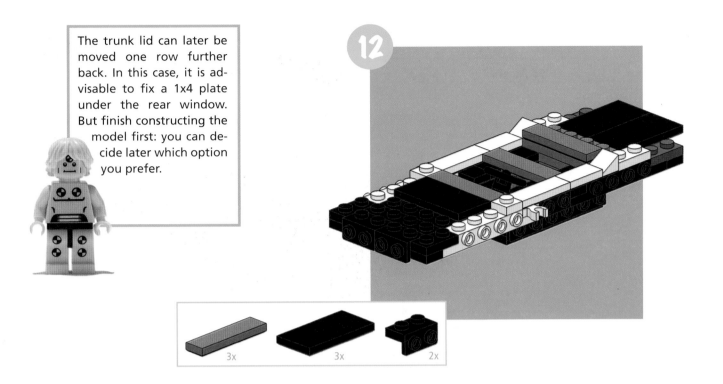

3x   3x   2x

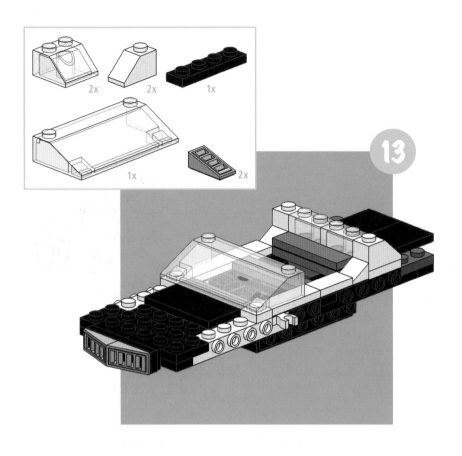

A keen observer would naturally notice that the vehicle's cooling ribs should run crosswise. But they also converge in the middle. Decide for yourself which version you prefer.

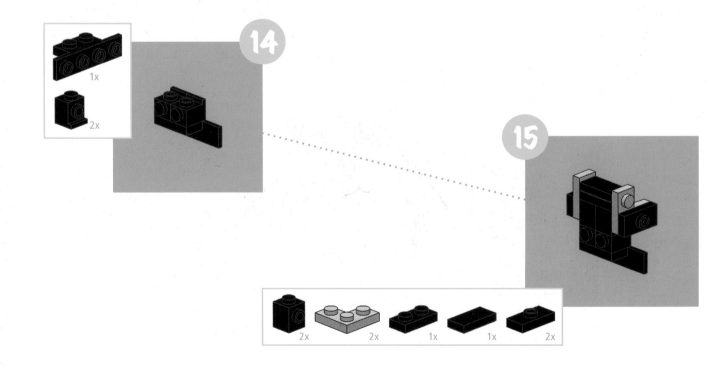

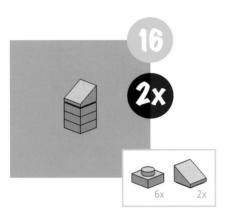

16

2x

6x 2x

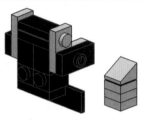

17

If you have only a limited supply of metallic silver and prefer not to order more, you can always vary the color. Light bluish gray is a good alternative.

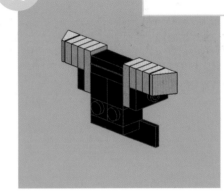

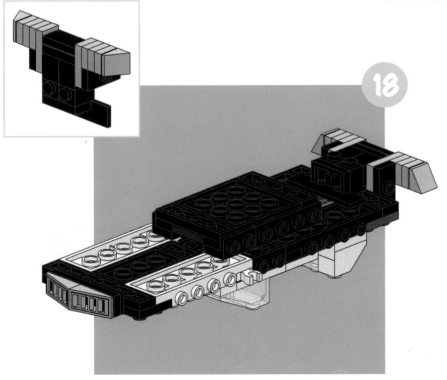

18

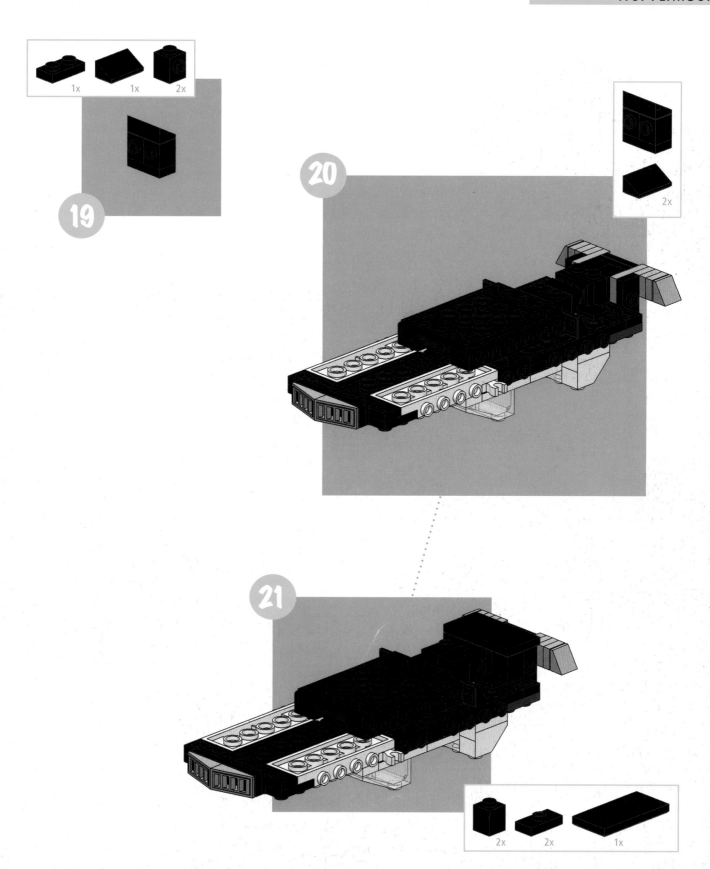

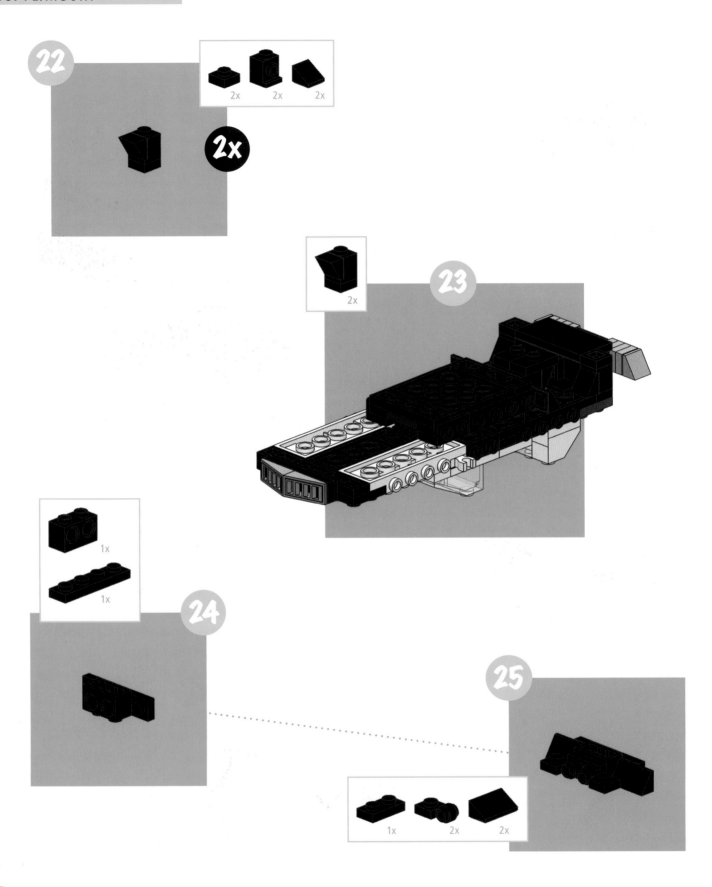

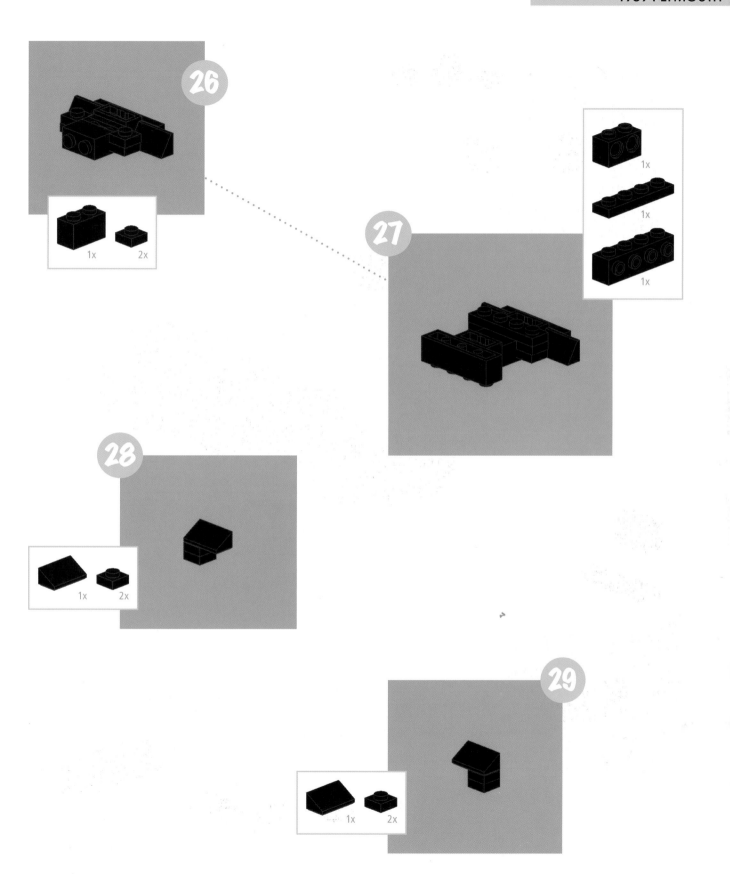

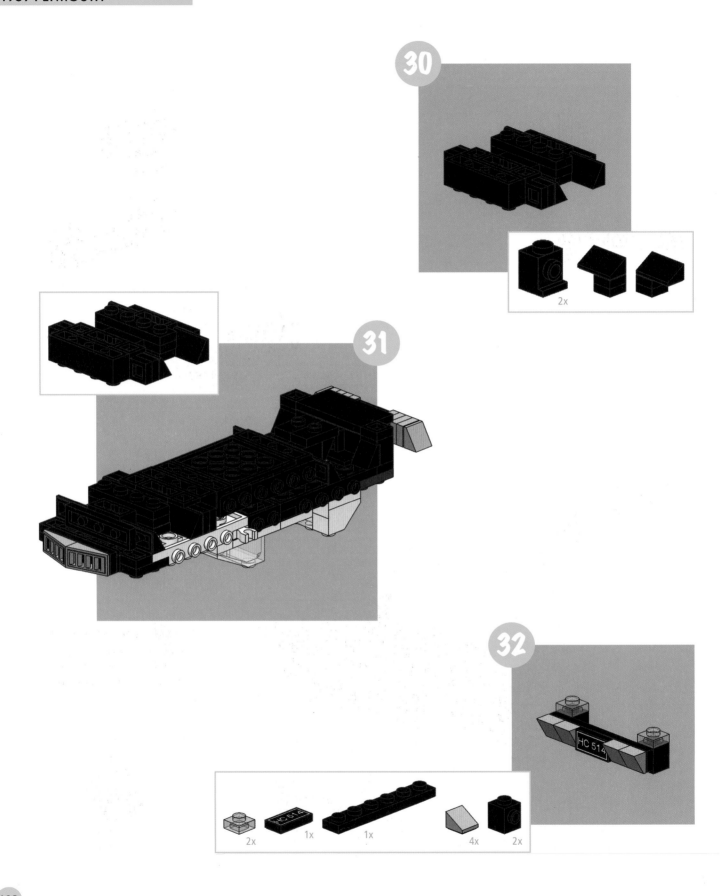

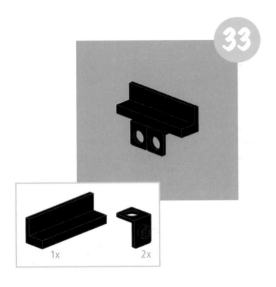

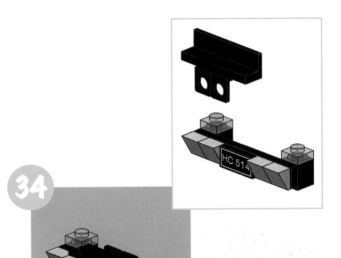

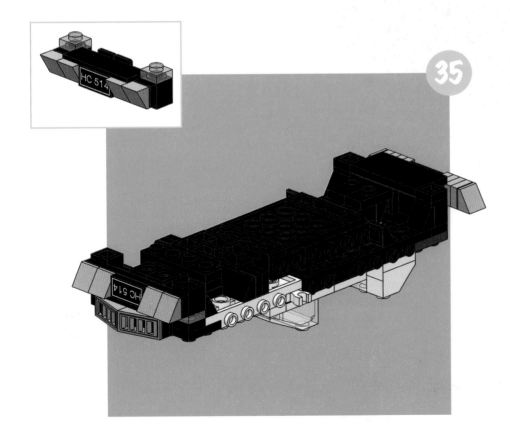

The 1x4 panel with the 2 neck brackets is not rigidly fixed so take care that it does not fall out during assembly.

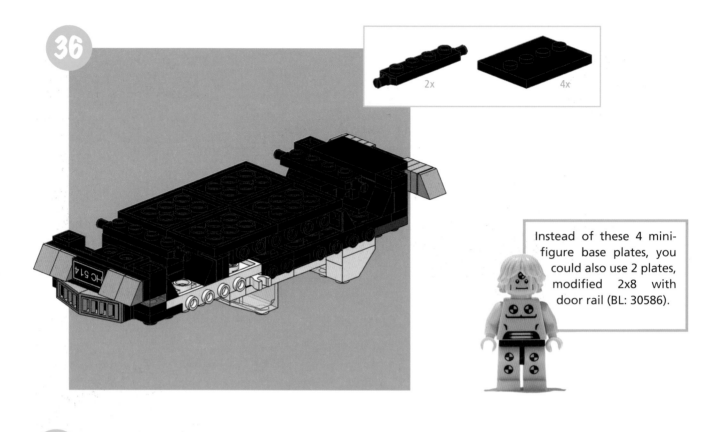

36

2x   4x

Instead of these 4 mini-figure base plates, you could also use 2 plates, modified 2x8 with door rail (BL: 30586).

37

1x   1x   2x   1x

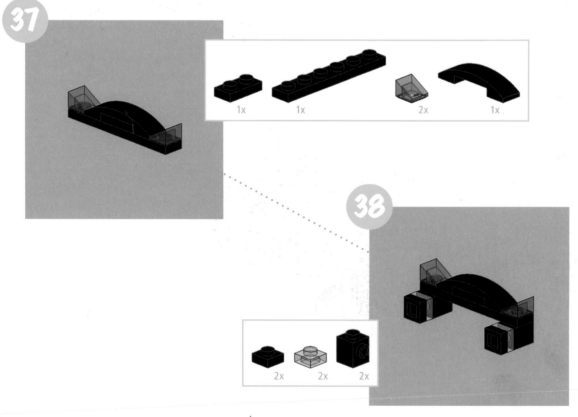

38

2x   2x   2x

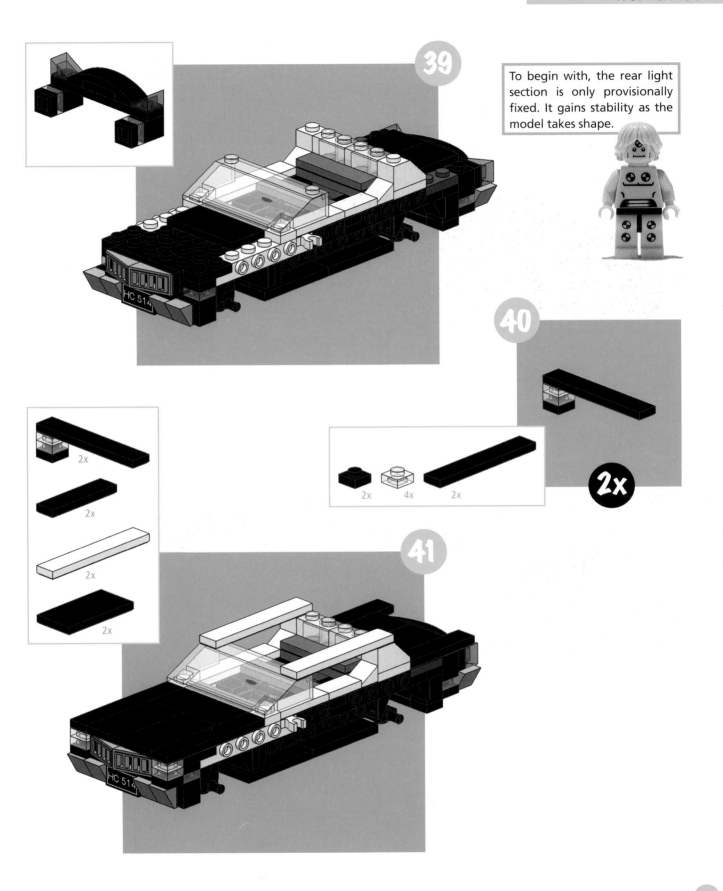

39

40

41

To begin with, the rear light section is only provisionally fixed. It gains stability as the model takes shape.

2x

2x

2x

2x

2x   4x   2x

2x

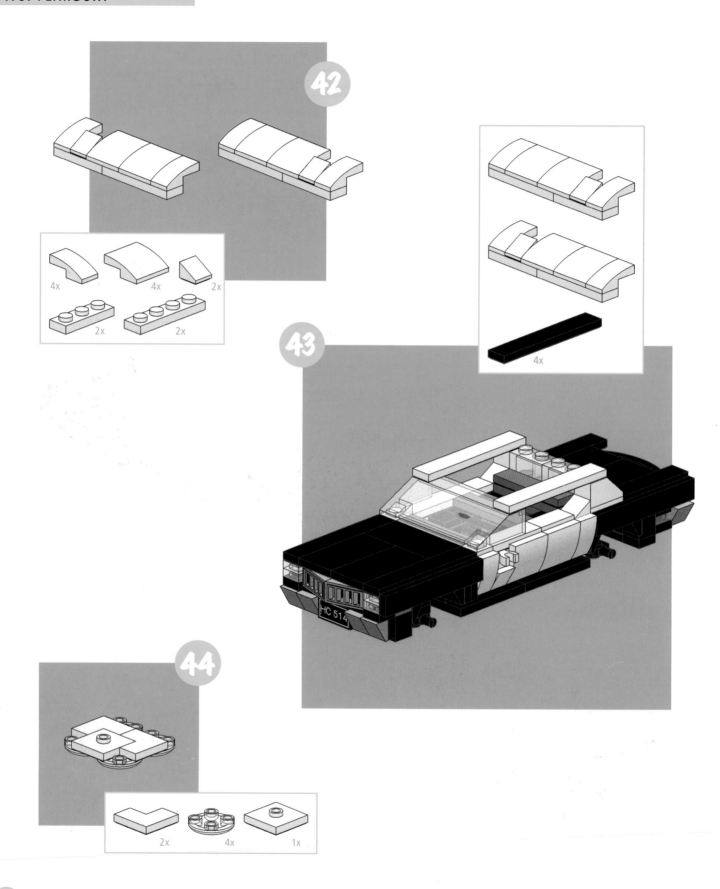

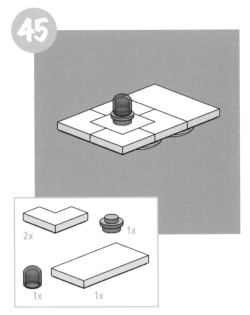

45

46

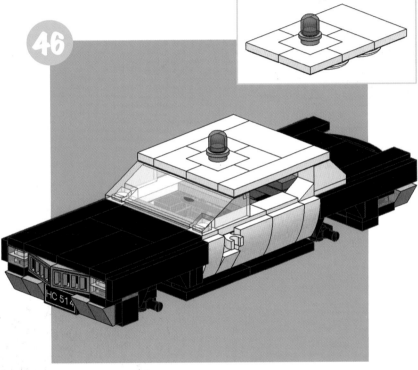

HC 514

47

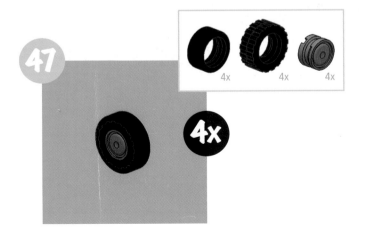

4x

The narrow racing tires are fitted over the other tires. Simply turn them inside out, knead them gently to warm up, and try not to nick them with your fingernails.

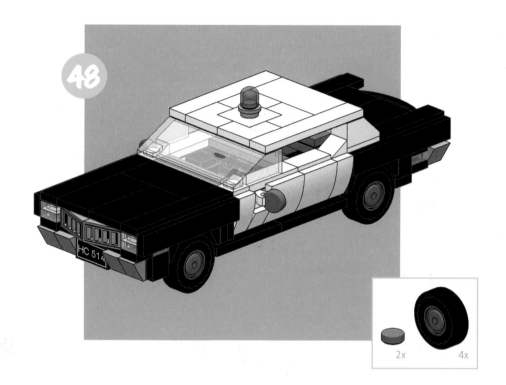

PARTS LIST

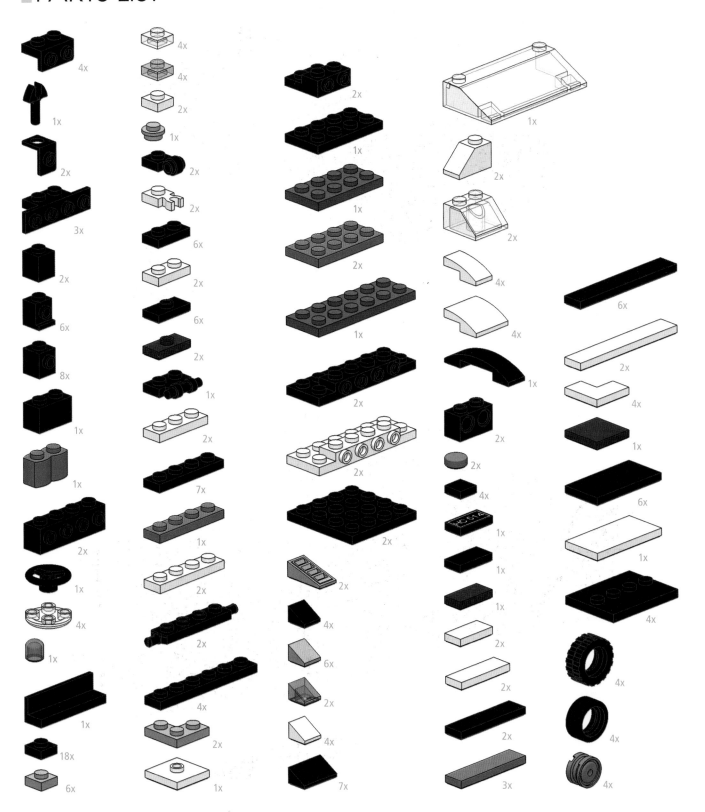

Quantity	Color	Element	Element Name	LEGO Code
4	Black	99781	Bracket 1 x 2 - 1 x 2 Down	6016172
1	Black	48729	Bar 1.5L with Clip	4289538
2	Black	42446	Bracket 1 x 1 - 1 x 1	4169047, 4261427, 6020192
3	Black	2436a	Bracket 1 x 2 - 1 x 4 Type 1	4282746
2	Black	3005	Brick 1 x 1	300526
6	Black	4070	Brick 1 x 1 with Headlight	407026
8	Black	87087	Brick 1 x 1 with Stud on 1 Side	4558954
1	Black	3004	Brick 1 x 2	300426
1	Dark Orange	30136	Brick 1 x 2 Log	4114054
2	Black	30414	Brick 1 x 4 with Studs on Side	4162443
1	Black	30663	Car Steering Wheel Large	4153044
4	Trans Clear	2654	Dish 2 x 2	4199303, 4278412
1	Trans Red	4773	Electric Light & Sound Colored Globe	unbekannt
1	Black	30413	Panel 1 x 4 x 1	4228063
18	Black	3024	Plate 1 x 1	302426
6	Metallic Silver	3024	Plate 1 x 1	4528732
4	Trans Clear	3024	Plate 1 x 1	3000840
4	Trans Orange	3024	Plate 1 x 1	4542673
2	White	3024	Plate 1 x 1	302401
1	Metallic Silver	4073	Plate 1 x 1 Round	4249039, 51809301
2	Black	4081b	Plate 1 x 1 with Clip Light Type 2	408126, 4632571
2	White	4085c	Plate 1 x 1 with Clip Vertical Type 3	408526, 4542319, 4550017
6	Black	3023	Plate 1 x 2	302326
2	White	3023	Plate 1 x 2	302301
6	Black	3794b	Plate 1 x 2 with Groove with 1 Centre Stud	379426
2	Reddish Brown	3794b	Plate 1 x 2 with Groove with 1 Centre Stud	4219726
1	Black	2540	Plate 1 x 2 with Handle	254026, 4140588
2	White	3623	Plate 1 x 3	362324
7	Black	3710	Plate 1 x 4	371026
1	Dark Orange	3710	Plate 1 x 4	4164448
2	White	3710	Plate 1 x 4	371001
2	Black	2926	Plate 1 x 4 with Wheels Holder	292626
4	Black	3666	Plate 1 x 6	366601
2	Metallic Silver	2420	Plate 2 x 2 Corner	4528731
1	White	87580	Plate 2 x 2 with Groove with 1 Center Stud	4565324
2	Black	99206	Plate 2 x 2 x 0.667 with Two Studs On Side and Two Raised	6052126
1	Black	3020	Plate 2 x 4	302026
1	Dark Bluish Gray	3020	Plate 2 x 4	4211065

Quantity	Color	Element	Element Name	LEGO Code
2	Dark Orange	3020	Plate 2 x 4	4164449, 4535928
1	Dark Bluish Gray	3795	Plate 2 x 6	4211002
2	Black	87609	Plate 2 x 6 x 0.667 with Four Studs On Side and Four Raised	4653049
2	White	87609	Plate 2 x 6 x 0.667 with Four Studs On Side and Four Raised	4560929
2	Black	3031	Plate 4 x 4	303126, 4243819
2	Metallic Silver	61409	Slope Brick 18 2 x 1 x 2/3 Grille	6092115
4	Black	54200	Slope Brick 31 1 x 1 x 2/3	4287159, 4504382
6	Metallic Silver	54200	Slope Brick 31 1 x 1 x 2/3	4528609
2	Trans Red	54200	Slope Brick 31 1 x 1 x 2/3	4244363
4	White	54200	Slope Brick 31 1 x 1 x 2/3	4244370, 4504369
7	Black	85984	Slope Brick 31 1 x 2 x 0.667	4548180
1	Trans Clear	58181	Slope Brick 33 3 x 6 without Inner Walls	4505359, 4542700
2	White	3040	Slope Brick 45 2 x 1	304001, 4121932
2	Trans Clear	3039	Slope Brick 45 2 x 2	622740
4	White	11477	Slope Brick Curved 2 x 1	6034044
4	White	15068	Slope Brick Curved 2 x 2 x 0.667	6047220
1	Black	93273	Slope Brick Curved 4 x 1 Double	4613153
2	Black	32000	Technic Brick 1 x 2 with Holes	3200026
2	Flat Silver	98138	Tile 1 x 1 Round with Groove	4655241
4	Black	3070b	Tile 1 x 1 with Groove	307026
1	Black	3069bpa1	Tile 1 x 2 with „HC514" Pattern	unbekannt
1	Black	3069b	Tile 1 x 2 with Groove	306926
1	Reddish Brown	3069b	Tile 1 x 2 with Groove	4211151
2	White	3069b	Tile 1 x 2 with Groove	306901
2	White	63864	Tile 1 x 3 with Groove	4558168
2	Black	2431	Tile 1 x 4 with Groove	243126
3	Dark Orange	2431	Tile 1 x 4 with Groove	6074893
6	Black	6636	Tile 1 x 6	663626
2	White	6636	Tile 1 x 6	663601
4	White	14719	Tile 2 x 2 Corner	6058329
1	Reddish Brown	3068b	Tile 2 x 2 with Groove	306826
6	Black	87079	Tile 2 x 4 with Groove	4560182
1	White	87079	Tile 2 x 4 with Groove	4560178
4	Black	88646	Tile 3 x 4 with Four Studs	4571146
4	Black	51011	Tyre 6.4/ 75 x 8 Shallow Offset Tread	4239237, 4515290, 4617848
4	Black	50945	Tyre 6/ 30 x 11	4246901
4	Flat Silver	93594	Wheel Rim 6.4 x 11 without Spokes	4624473

45-DEGREE ANGLE

The original plan for our car park installation envisaged incorporating one parking area at a 45-degree angle to the others. We resolved this situation by fitting a separate, preconstructed section into the surface area of the set. The important thing is, to avoid snagging or tilting, to make sure that the inserted section rests on a smooth, stud-free surface. The edges also have to be as smooth as possible. The whole area is fixed at the sides and clipped together by the following pieces: wedge plate 3x3 cut corner (BL: 2450), wedge plate 4x4 cut corner (BL: 30503), wedge plate 6x6 cut corner (BL: 6106), and wedge plate 8x8 cut corner (BL: 30504). Because the wedge plates are cut to size at the corners of the 45° section, they have to be laid in two overlapping layers so that no gaps into the substructure are left.

ZOMBIE ATTACK

This zombie attack marks the end of our car park scenes. The "control the action" explosion was constructed, as mentioned earlier, in a diorama. It is also worth noting at this point that all the components used are original LEGO pieces. As always, no colors were changed and nothing was modified using any non-LEGO parts. The explosion is shown again as a separate image. And once more as seen from below. This construction method can be used to represent a hemisphere and alter the angles as required.

ALL-TERRAIN VEHICLE

I was inspired to build this car by the latest Mad Max movie, though it is not directly based on a specific model. I simply wanted to see what could be done with the movie's famous apocalyptic setting. The result is shown on the preceding double page. I am a great fan of cars, robots, spaceships, etc., anything that looks as if it has been randomly assembled. It was therefore imperative to create something in this style.

Initially, I tried out various ideas using the new rims of the Speed Champions construction sets. I came to the conclusion, however, that these just looked too new and pristine, which is why I decided on these other alternatives.

The rear of this car was modified to provide space for all the equipment that might be needed for survival purposes: fuel, floodlights, tools, spare tires,

even a fire extinguisher. After all, you never know …

The external projections at the front are defined by the two panels (BL: 4865 in light bluish grey, LEGO: 4211515). Since the vehicle is seven studs in width, a 1x6 plate fits between the two panels on which the headlights and radiator grille are mounted. The 1x6 plate can be shifted half a stud with the aid of jumper elements (BL: 3794 in dark bluish grey, LEGO: 4211119).

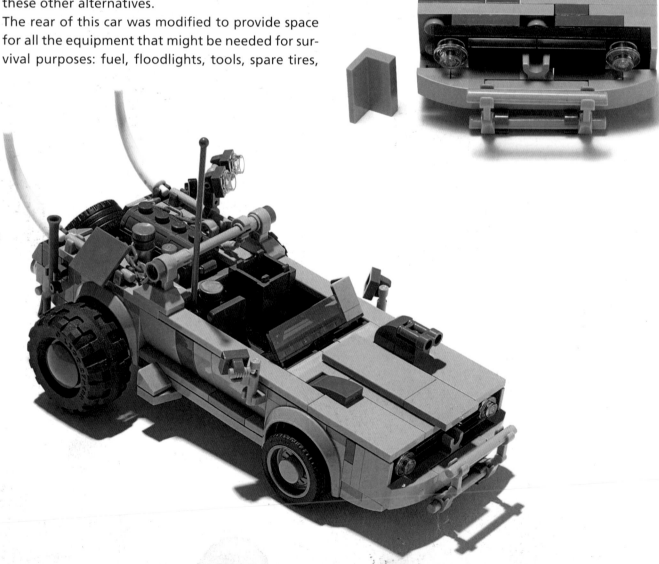

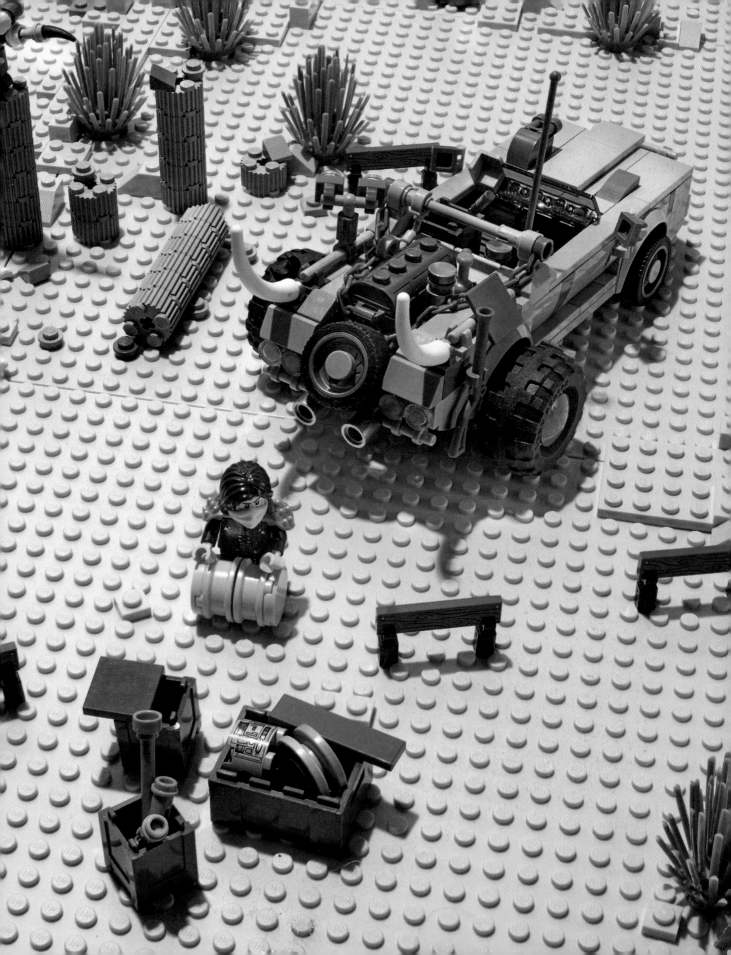

VULTURE

Everyone likes to experiment with something new. I have always been interested in constructing small-scale models—the smaller the better. I soon hit upon the idea of trying my hand at a vulture. Vultures do after all have a very distinctive shape and posture and I had rarely seen one as a LEGO model. I used the horns of a Star Wars Tauntaun for the wings (BL: 86057 in tan, LEGO: 4550314). The neck is made from a laser sword handle (BL: 61199 in light bluish grey, LEGO: 4527160), fixed diagonally into the clip of a 1x1 plate, modified. The vulture's legs (BL: 11090 in dark bluish grey, LEGO: 6015890) are also fixed by somewhat unconventional means as the element is inserted from below into the 1x1 plate. Despite this, both the neck and legs stay in position surprisingly well.

PORSCHE MODEL SERIES

As you will discover later in this book, railways are my overriding passion. Joe nevertheless suggested at some point that I might want to try something new so, after giving this a little thought, I decided on a Porsche 911. After fiddling around for a while, I came up with the results shown below and also on the next double page. From right to left: a 1971 Porsche 911 S Coupé in black, a 1973 Porsche 911 Carrera RS 2.7 Coupé in yellow, followed by a 1980 Porsche 911 SC Coupé in red. A distinctive feature at the front is the deep, curved hood between the two raised, circular headlights. This was constructed using slope curved 2x2 no studs (BL: 15068) for the hood and the Technic liftarm 1x2, thick (BL: 43857) to mount the headlights. Anyone who is familiar with the early Porsche models will certainly be aware of the many different types of wheel rim. Starting off with small rims and tires with high sidewalls (so-called Fuchs rims), they changed later to the deep-dish style, wide tread and shorter sidewall. But how to reproduce this in a LEGO model? The new Speed Champions sets with the right sort of rims and wheel covers were perfect in this respect. The photo shows tire 14 mm D. x 6 mm Solid Smooth (BL: 50945) fitted on wheel 18 mm D. x 12 mm with axle hole and black stud (BL: 18976), including Wheel Cover 7 Spoke Y Shape in flat silver (BL: 18979b) as a Fuchs rim on the black Porsche. I used the same tire on the same rim with Wheel Cover 5 Spoke in flat silver (BL: 18978a) as the combination for the yellow Porsche. And the red version also has the same tire, but this time, because of its deep-dish effect, on the wheel without a wheel cover in flat silver.

What people automatically associate with a Porsche are the rear spoilers. I made the large spoiler on the red Porsche by fixing a hinge Train Gate 2x4 black (BL: 2873) to a Hinge Tile 1x4 red (BL: 4645). The small spoiler on the yellow vehicle was made from the following elements: Slope 30 1x1x2/3 yellow (BL: 54200, or alternatively BL: 50746) and Slope 30 1x2x2/3 yellow (BL: 85984).

APM 1904

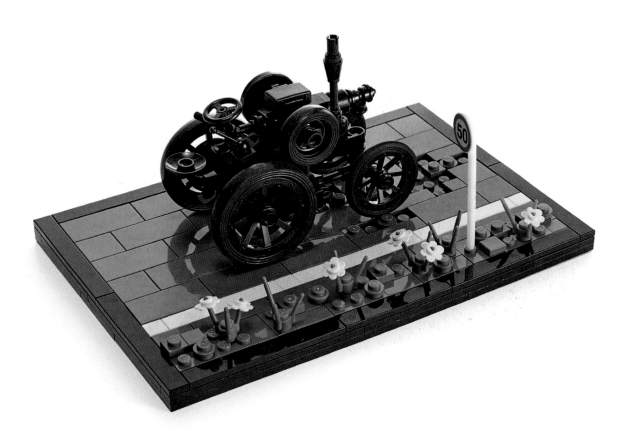

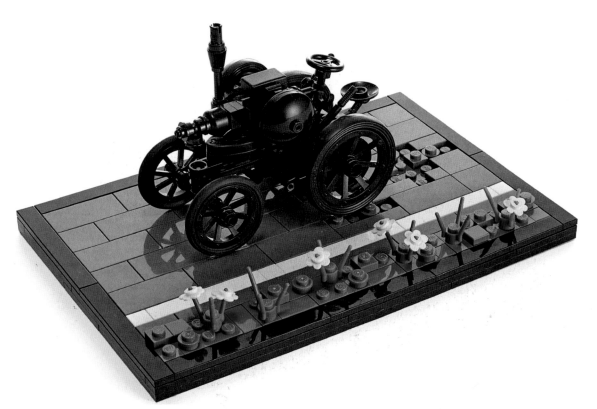

LANZ BULLDOG HL 12 PS

To mark his boss's forthcoming major birthday, a friend commissioned me to construct a Lanz Bulldog. I imagined this would be a task quickly accomplished. Uwe was visiting at the time so we started a kind of competition whereby we took an old model by Misterzumbi and tried to freshen it up using new elements. We finished up with a result that was completely different, a model that combined the best ideas from all three of us. All in all, it took around two weeks though, every day, we thought we had finished the project only to end up making further changes. We were particularly delighted by the recipient's appreciative reaction since he is a collector of real Lanz Bulldog tractors and therefore a real expert.

The base element of this Lanz Bulldog HL 12 PS, pictured left as Iron Bulldog (farm tractor) and right as Traffic Bulldog (road version), is a Technic liftarm 1x7 thin black (BL: 32065). The respective elements are fixed to this below and above. For a more detailed view, we have divided up the model as shown right into an exploded-view photo. The only construction difference between the two versions is the type of tires on the rear wheels. The Traffic Bulldog has wheel wagon large 33 mm D., undetermined hole type (BL: 4489) fitted with Smooth Old Style Large tire (BL: 36). The Iron Bulldog, on the other hand, has 17 links of Technic link chain black (BL: 3711).

The front wheels comprise wheel wagon small 27 mm D. (BL: 2470) with Technic wedge belt wheel tires (BL: 2815, alternatively BL: 70162). Hose rigid 3 mm D.6L 4.8 cm black (BL: 75c06) was used for the front axles and hose rigid 3 mm D.3L 5.6 cm black (BL: 75c07) for the rear. More frequent use was made of the new 1x1 round plate with open stud in black (BL: 85861), for example as a fixing for the wheels which allows them to rotate, or even as a cover for the tractor nose in combination with the new-style, pneumatic T-piece (BL: 4697b black).

An example of "nice part usage" is the black briefcase on top of the Bulldog (minifig utensil briefcase, BL: 4449), utilized here to represent a square fuel tank. Or the black Technic Pin (Technic Pin ½ black, BL: 4274) forming the end of the exhaust pipe, not to mention the black 1x1 plate clip type 1 (modified with vertical thin open O clip, black, BL: 4085a) as a single fixing, inserted in a slope inverted 33 3x1 black (BL: 4287) for the steering wheel unit. Or the spoked wheels, which usually used as carriage wheels.

LANZ BULLDOG VARIATIONS

Left: Lanz Bulldog HN3-D7506
Right: Lanz Bulldog HN2-12/20
These are the actual descriptions of the two models. Both are constructed in dark bluish gray. Let us concentrate first on the tractor on the right because, if we begin by understanding the construction method of the smaller vehicle, the secrets of the large one will become clear. To give you a more detailed view, we have presented this model in an exploded-view photo.

Unsurprisingly, this MOC likewise involves frequent use of the new 1x1 round plate with hole in black (BL: 85861) – in this instance, specifically in combination with a hose rigid 3 mm D.3L 2.4 cm (BL: 75c03) as an antiroll bar for the cab as well as for attaching the steering wheel. In addition, this combination of parts is used at the rear of the tractor for attaching the fender, while this small part is also used to connect the hand brake. The hand brake itself consists of a black screwdriver (minifig utensil tool screwdriver narrow head black, BL: 6246a) inserted into a hose rigid 3 mm D.1L 0.8 cm black (BL: 75c01), which in turn is fitted into a bar holder with a black clip (BL: 11090). The entire section is then attached to the cab wall, a 2x2 tile (dark bluish gray, BL: 3068) by means of a small piece of rigid hose 3 mm black—inserted into a 1x1 round plate with hole.

Of particular note is the model's rotatable front axle and rear wheels. In the illustration, we have separated out these components to show the construction in closer detail.

The two rear wheels consist of: a Technic bush 1/2 smooth black (BL: 4265c), a hose rigid 3 mm D.5L 4.0 cm black (BL: 75c05), a wheel wagon large 33 mm D, undetermined hole type black (BL: 4498), a tire 30.4x14 VR Balloon black (BL: 2994, or alternatively BL: 6578), a Technic wedge belt wheel (pulley) red (BL: 4185) and a 2x2 inverted radar dish red (BL: 4740). Please note: the soft tire gets its rounded shape solely from being fitted onto a spoked wheel (diameter 33 mm).

The front axle consists of: two 2x2 inverted radar dishes red (BL: 4740), two tires Smooth Old Style small black (BL: 132), two wheels, spoked 2x2 with pin hole black (BL: 30155), two Technic pins 1/2 light bluish gray (BL: 4274), two round plates 1x1 with open stud black (BL: 85861), as well as a hose rigid 3 mm D.7L 5.6 cm black (BL: 75c07). To reproduce the visual appearance of the wheel cover, it is important that only a minimal amount of tire from the rim touches the 2x2 dish. Too much and the dish—which is firmly fixed to the hose rigid 3 mm—will block the rim from moving freely due to the Technic pin 1/2 attached to the hose.

The individual pieces are shown—in each case from foot to top—on the exploded-view photo.

STEAM LOCOMOTIVE S2/5

This scene showcases my model of steam engine S2/5 of the Royal Bavarian State Railway (RBSR) in the state colors of black and blue. It is motorized by the LEGO Power Functions System (PF): in short, the PF Train Motor in the engine (BL: 88002), and the PF IR Receiver (BL: 8884) and PF Rechargeable Battery Box (BL: 8878) in the tender. The reason for building this Atlantic-type express steam locomotive was that it has just two coupled drive axles out of a total of five axles (hence its classification, S2/5). A further consideration was its two-axle bogie (front axle).

Atlantic-type steam towing tender locomotives are classified as 2'B1 or 2'B1' depending on wheel arrangement, i.e. locomotives with a front bogie or front axle (where 2 stands for two-axle), two coupled drive axles (B), and a towing or running axle (1), which is either rigidly fixed in the frame or movably mounted.

When constructing a steam engine model, in this case one with a tow tender, it is important—once you have decided whether to build an actual engine or an imaginary version—to work out which of the two possible construction methods to use. Should it be a working model or purely decorative? Nonworking models are relatively straightforward and you can just get on with building them.

In the case of a working model, you will also need to decide between two further options: a pusher engine, which is driven by an external motor on one of the carriages behind the engine, or a self-powered model, like my Bavarian S2/5. The following applies to whichever choice you make: build the engine chassis first and test its drivability within the LEGO track radius with points and S-curves. Once you are satisfied with this, you can begin assembling the locomotive. There is nothing more frustrating than having created a beautiful steam engine only to find that it keeps derailing all the time on its maiden run and turns out to be undrivable.

The engine chassis for both versions is divided into three sections: beginning at the front with the bogie, or front axle, followed by the section containing the large drive wheels (or drive axles) and finally the so-called towing or running axle. The three parts are connected by a pivot at the front and rear of the middle drive wheel section. In short, this rule of thumb applies to all LEGO steam engines of this type. In the LEGO track radius, a rigid construction requires a swivel-action undercarriage which is fixed at two points. The freedom of movement of the front and towing axle is protected by tiles (stud-free and smooth) mounted on top of them towards the body of the engine. The firm connection between the engine body and chassis is provided exclusively by the middle drive axle section.

An equally important factor is the minimum distance of one stud (LEGO unit of measurement 1L = 0.8 cm) between the end of the engine and the towing tender, so that the end of the locomotive does not get caught up with the turning tender as it swings out

whenever the train rounds a curve (cf. photo).

The picture also shows the freely visible swivel-mounted towing axle as well as the movable fixing point connecting the tender to the engine. This consists of the following LEGO parts: plate modified 3x2 with hole black (BL: 3176, 1 x) on the towing axle, one Technic axle 2 black (BL: 3704), two Technic bushes 1/2 smooth light bluish gray (BL: 4265c), as well as one Technic plate 1x6 with toothed ends black (BL: 4262). Also visible is the connecting cable between the PF Train Motors (BL: 88002) and the PF IR Receiver (BL: 8884). The cable should have a fairly wide arch to provide flexibility whenever the end of the engine swings in and out.

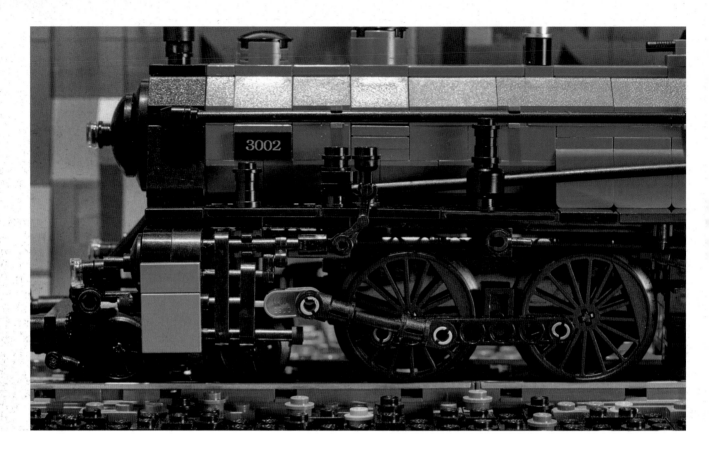

Let us now look at the connecting rod arrangement, which is both technically and visually an important feature of a steam locomotive. For a more delicate effect, I always use a combination of Technic liftarm thin and Technic plate. In this case, given the distance between the pin holes of the two spoked wheels, the purpose was served by a Technic liftarm 1x7 thin black (BL: 32065) combined with two Technic pins 3/4 dark bluish gray (BL: 32002). Further along towards the steam cylinder are two Technic pins 1/2 light bluish gray (BL: 4274), two Technic axle and pin connector toggle joint elements smooth black (BL: 44), with a piece of hose rigid 3 mm D.3L 2.4 cm black (BL: 75c03) inserted into these, as well as a Technic flex cable end pin connection dark gray (BL: 2900) with a Technic flex cable (stud measure) 7L light gray (BL: bb08c07L). To feed the Technic flex cable in the cylinder, I used one brick modified 1x1 with studs on two sides black (BL: 47905) and one brick 1x1 with hole black (BL: 6541). To prevent the Technic flex cable getting caught up by the two LEGO bricks during operation, a piece of hose rigid 3 mm D.3L 2.4 cm black (BL: 75c03) was used as a kind of guide tube with, for optical reasons, a hose flexible 8.5L, end 1 x 1 x 2/3 tabless black (BL: 752) fitted over the end of it.

The photo also shows the two-axle, pivoted bogie (double front axle). It should be mentioned at this point that it is connected from above by way of a centered pivot, designed to help it round bends easily. A single-axle bogie generally needs no more than some kind of rigid connection. An important factor in both types, however, is the pressure point from above. If this is not properly taken into account during the engine's construction, the front axle could derail, e.g. if the train encounters any bumps or points. Neither should you overlook the correct distance between the right and left steam cylinder, in relation to the pivoted bogie. For example, if this follows the track direction when rounding a curve to the left, the rigid engine construction will swing out to the right.

On the subject of "nice part usage," the upturned blue seats encasing the boiler and running toward the engine driver's cab, as well as black garden fences forming the running grille (BL: 3185 fence 1x4x2 black; cf. photo) should be noted. The holes in the fence panels also serve as fixing points for various boiler attachments.

The integration of the blue seats—minifig utensil seat 2x2 blue (BL: 4079) as well as minifig utensil seat 2x2 with center sprue mark blue (BL: 4079b)—also warrants a closer look. The main construction element in this respect is the Technic plate 1x6 with toothed ends black (BL: 4262). A double row of these running parallel to one another are fixed in position with a tile (tile 2x4 black, BL: 87079) at the top and a plate (BL: 3020 plate 2x4 black) underneath. The blue seats are stuck onto the black 2x4 plate and the spaces at either end filled with a tile (BL: 3069b tile 1x2 with groove black). The resulting construction is now turned over and pressed firmly onto the unit pictured in the center of the photo, which has been assembled as shown. The whole section can then be attached to the model. I still make the occasional steam engine with towing tender and I hope you will too.

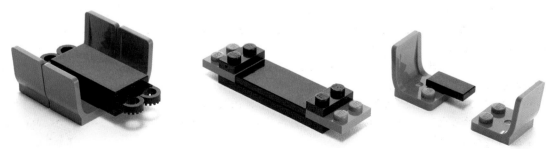

KÖF II

A shunting engine, diesel locomotive, perhaps even a Köf or something a bit bigger? All these ideas whizz around my head. Eventually, it turned into an entire series, starting with Kö I to Kö II and then to Köf II and III. Representative of all these, the photo shows my Köf II pushing a flatbed wagon colored red/black (BL color). The name Köf II indicates a small locomotive with an oil-powered motor and fluid drive in performance group 2 (50–150 HP). This powerful little German Railways (Deutsche Bundesbahn, DB) engine dating from the early 1930s to the late 1950s is powered by the old 9V train motor (electric train motor 9V modern, BL: 590, or alternatively BL: 70358).

The use of various LEGO elements for purposes other than their original function once again played a major role in this MOC ("my own creation") model. Starting with the syringe in light gray (BL: 87989 minifig utensil syringe light bluish gray) used as a dipstick in the engine compartment, the light gray binoculars (BL: 30162 minifig utensil binoculars town light bluish gray) combined with the telescope in light gray (BL: 64644 minifig utensil telescope light bluish gray) on the roof as a signal, the hands both in light gray as a door handle and in black as a shut-off valve (BL: 983 hand light bluish gray and black), plus minifig neck brackets with stud in red and black (BL: 42446) as headlight holders.

The plate modified 1x1 with horizontal thick open O clip (BL: 61252), inserted into the stud space of a LEGO brick, can often be an invisible fixing option. With this model, the method is used for mounting the compressed air container of the braking system at the front of the engine (details in the foreground of the photo).

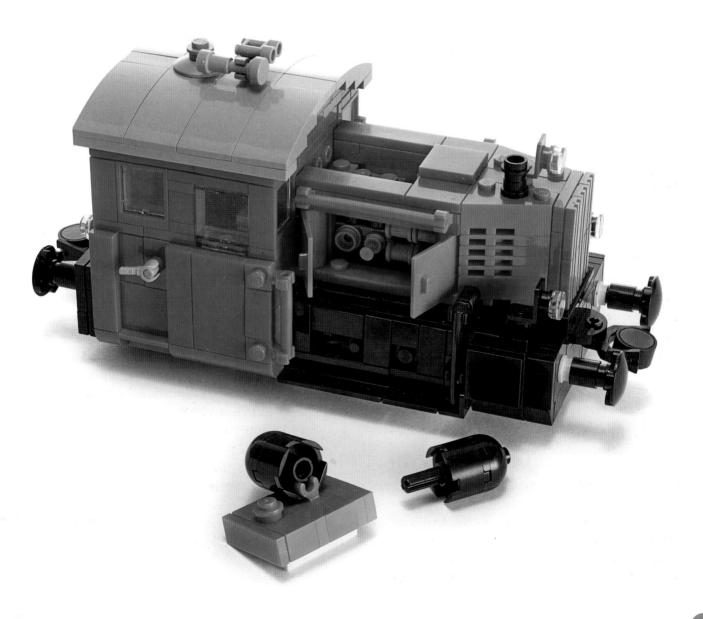

FLATBED RAILWAY WAGON

Goods wagons or carriages should be part of every train scenario. We will now show you how one basic construction can be used as the base for various types of wagon. First of all, lay two Technic plates 1x6 with toothed ends black (BL: 4262) parallel to each other. Then, press the brown bracket BL: 2436 (bracket 1x2–1x4 brown, as reddish-brown is rare), studs facing downwards, into the adjacent pinholes of the Technic plates (SNOT technique). You can see from the photo how the rest of this flatbed wagon is assembled. It is interesting and also important to know where the red rod comes from which joins the 1x1 bricks (BL: 3005 1x1 reddish-brown), which face each other at the front and back ends of the wagon. As described at the very beginning of this book, a Technic axle can be used to push it out of an old hinge element (BL: 3149c01 hinge plate 2x5 complete assembly or BL: 3324c01 hinge plate 2x9 complete assembly, where it functioned as a connecting rod between two hinge sections.

It is also a general rule with regard to LEGO track radius that fixed axles should be a maximum of 8–9 studs apart in order to guarantee the stability of a moving wagon. If the distance is any greater, the wagon would likely derail when traveling around curves. However, in the case of our MOC model, in which there are far more than the maximum number of 8–9 studs, we have resorted to a little trick: we made the axles movable with the aid of a turntable (BL: 3680c002 turntable 2x2 plate, complete assembly with light bluish gray top) and stretched an appropriately sized rubber belt between the two axles—here the rubber belt medium round cross section approx. 3x3 blue (BL: x37). The effect of this is that tension in the rubber belt causes the axles to straighten up on their own after rounding a curve.

In addition to a flatbed wagon, other similar wagons can be made from this basic design, such as stake cars or low side cars. Why not just try some out!

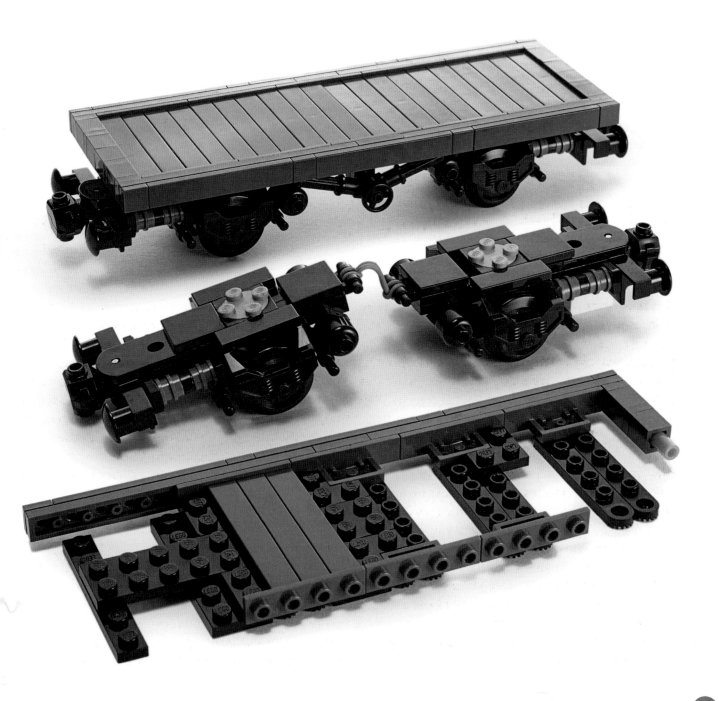

Y-WING

An absolute Star Wars classic! This Y-Wing combines a large number of details in a very small model. It is a LEGO micro-scale construction. And yes, I really love building on this scale!

I must admit that it took a moment before I hit upon the idea of using rubber bands to represent the yellow stripes around the nose of the engines. Obviously these were not just ordinary bands but obtained from LEGO sets (BL: x90yellow, LEGO: 4544151). They fit the purpose better than anything else I tried.

At first glance, the detailed picture of the cockpit does not seem particularly exciting but some of you may notice that I have combined three brackets here in an interesting arrangement. Brackets are brilliant! You can do all kinds of things with them even in the most limited space.

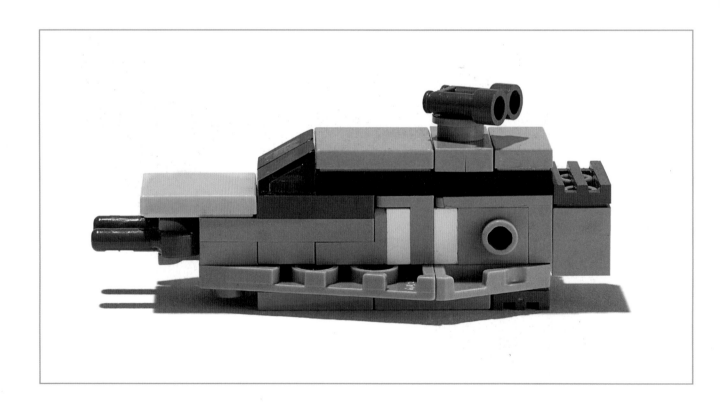

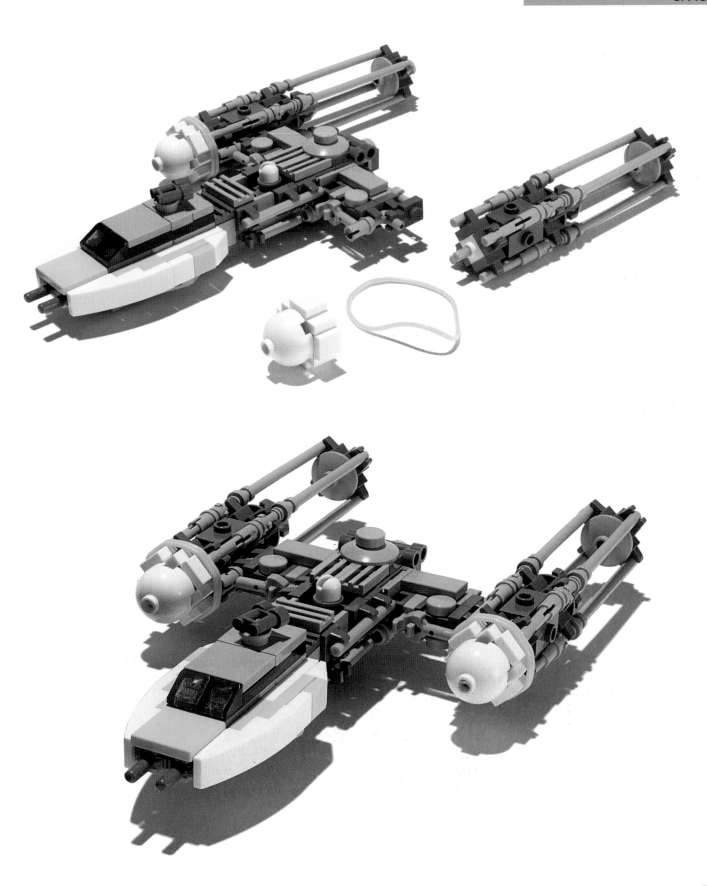

LAAT GUNSHIP

Here is another Star Wars model in micro-scale style. I really had great fun building the famous LAAT Gunship as I wanted to incorporate its distinctive shape and its most important features in "my own creation" (MOC). All the guns and other weapons can be positioned wherever you want them and even the slightly angled doors can be closed. The printed transparent windscreens are an official LEGO element (BL: 4740pb005 in trans-clear, LEGO: 4657615). The little figure is a Snowtrooper, by the way: not entirely authentic but the best option for imitating a clone (unfortunately not available as a LEGO character).

The exploded-view photo shows that the front of the guns consists of a Technic pin with spherical head (BL: 6628 in light bluish gray, LEGO: 4158312) and a 1x2 plate with clips (BL: 60470 in light bluish gray, LEGO: 4515173). LEGO itself has meanwhile used this construction technique several times. Most people have probably only come across the spherical-headed Technic pin in black since only two sets feature it in light bluish gray.

I used a spanner wrench (BL: 6246d dark gray) in order to keep the connection between the guns and the ship as delicate as possible whilst still allowing movement. As a result, the tower can be swiveled both horizontally and vertically. This former style of

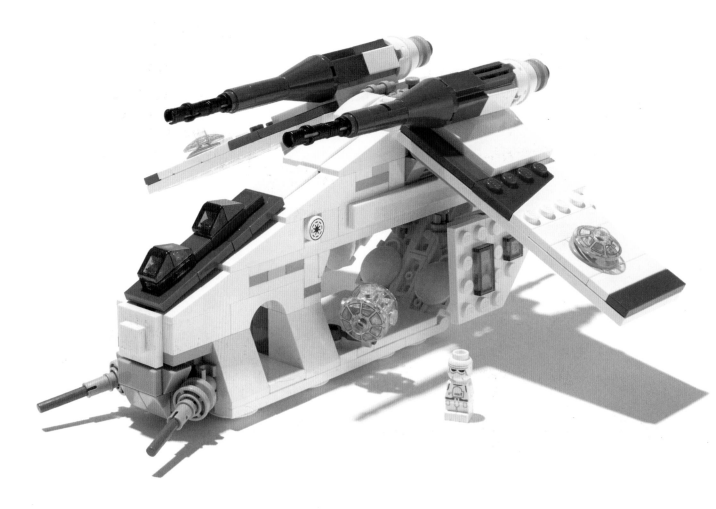

spanner wrench has since been changed to a more modern version but this is not available in the color I want, which is why I opted for the older version. The photos also clearly show how the doors are held by a Droid arm in light gray (BL: 30377 in light bluish gray, LEGO: 4211658).

To install the angled doors, I used laser sword handles that had been slightly bowed (BL: 61199 in light bluish gray, LEGO: 4527160). These create the perfect angle for fitting the doors to the body of the ship. They are stabilized by a third Droid arm that simultaneously keeps the handles at the correct distance for attaching them from below onto a three-stud base.

Anyone who is wondering how the cockpit is attached can see in the detailed photo how this was done. The difficult aspect of this task was to preserve as far as possible a sealed, unbroken surface. This method meant I could create the right angle as well as a smooth transition to the rest of the ship.

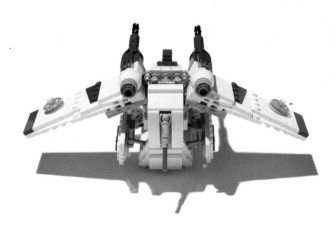

AT-ST

Everyone knows the AT-ST Walker from Star Wars! Even when I was constructing models for the book "Build Your Own Galaxy," I really enjoyed making micro-scale models. The smaller the model, the more difficult it becomes to transfer the details of the original subject but, as a great Star Wars fan, there was no way I could neglect the classic AT-ST Walker. Its most distinctive feature is undoubtedly the head: the unusually shaped viewing slits were practically begging to be replicated.

It goes without saying that the rear has been constructed to resemble the original as closely as possible and provides a useful view of how the legs are constructed. The upper and lower legs are linked by a joint which snaps into place, providing more stability. Heels and toes are linked by flat joints in order to compensate for any uneven surface. The legs can be fully rotated 360°.

The inner workings of AT-ST took me some time. The most difficult task was to fix the plates on the sides. Each side is attached to the head by a single stud; the two sides are linked together again by another single stud. The third stud, which you can see in the photo, supports a 1x2 tile.

The exploded view of the head displays the connecting piece that joins the two sides together and the laser guns in the center. These consist of two pairs of binoculars fixed together end to end (BL: 30162 in dark bluish gray, LEGO: 4211051) and two bars with clips (BL: 48729b in dark bluish gray, LEGO: 4289542).

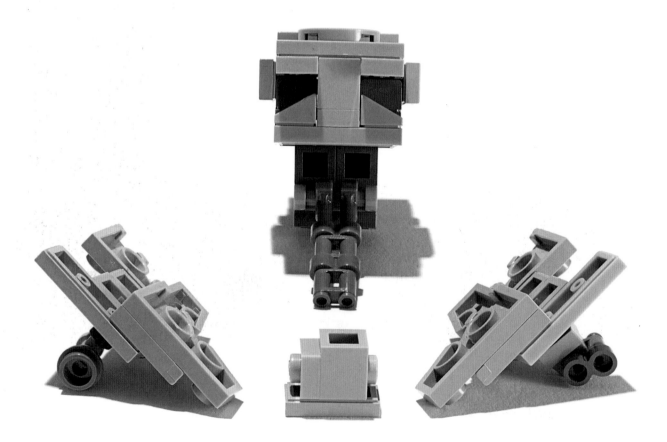

RACER

This unarmed ship is intended for racing over the surface of planets, similar to the Star Wars Podracer. Like the Podracer, its equipment is kept to the absolute minimum: a very open cockpit for maximum visibility, as well as room for the pilot as well as a navigator, a long nose to make it at least a bit aerodynamic and, naturally, two giant engines that can take the ship to breakneck speeds. Note the snow flurries caused by the engines! I had this model standing on a shelf for a long time but was never quite satisfied with it. I was constantly trying out alterations but it has gradually assumed a shape I like.

I am not a great fan of stickers but I will make an exception if they are used for the pieces for which they were intended. In this instance, both the stickers and the pieces they decorate all come from Set 7712 of the Exo Force series.

I have attached small auxiliary engines to the sides of the wings to increase maneuverability in case the racer suddenly has to evade an obstacle. For the frontal view, we removed the windshield to allow a glimpse inside the cockpit. The pilot (in front) naturally handles the control levers whilst the navigator (behind) has a small display area and flat work space.

And here is another interesting construction technique: the pieces we refer to as cheese graters (BL: 61409 yellow, LEGO: 4521167) can be fixed under certain plates and bricks using the hand of a minifigure. This presents a wide range of possibilities for rounding off unattractive edges.

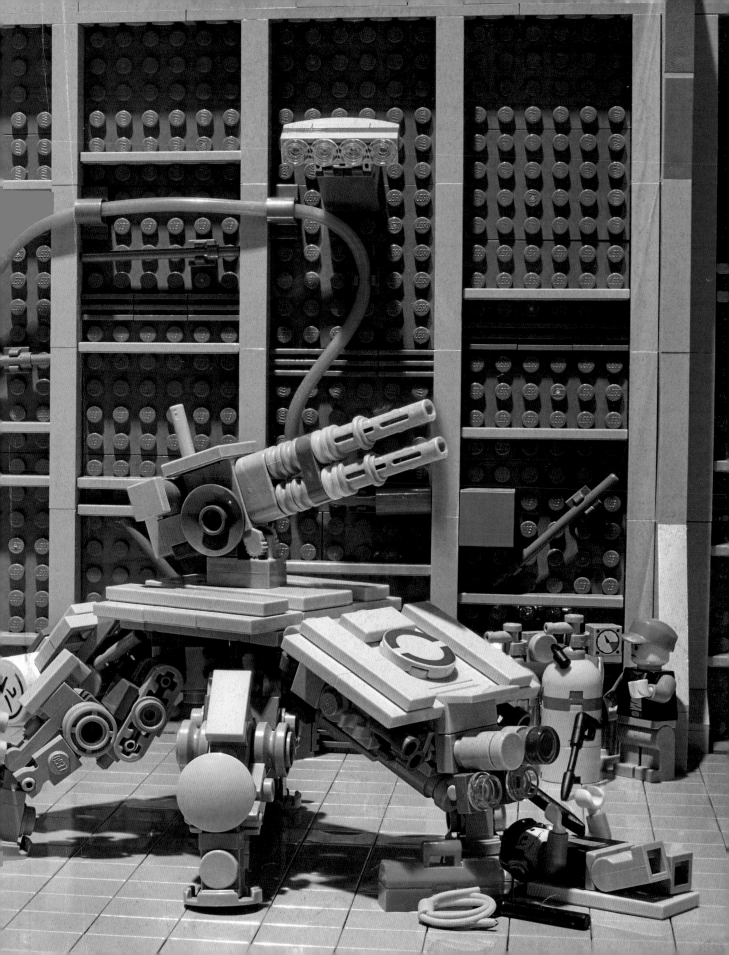

MECHA

The four legs of this Mech seem rigid but they are actually more movable than appearances might suggest. You can put the Mech into almost any position you want without compromising its stability. An uneven base does not pose a problem. The photos of the underneath and the leg of the Mech clearly show how they are constructed.

The legs are fixed to the body as follows: the cross formed by the brick modified and plate modified, turned 45°, fits perfectly into the round holes on the underside of a 4x4 plate, or larger one. The holding strength of this combination is incredible!

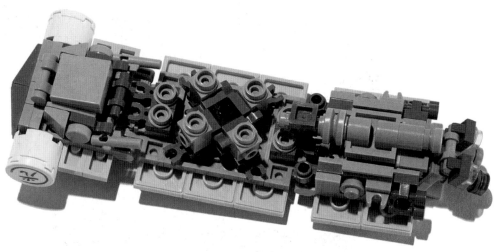

MECHA

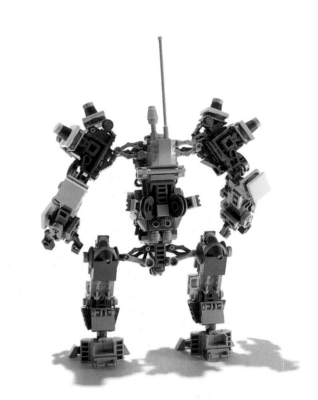

Here is an interesting suggestion for fixing arms and legs. The elements with BrickLink numbers 30377 and 4735 should imitate a kind of hydraulic action. Although this keeps arms and legs a good distance from the body, it does guarantee considerable freedom of movement.

It is easier to see the distances between body and limbs more clearly against a white background. The arms can be moved and swiveled at the shoulder, elbow and wrist joints, as required. The sides and front of the pilot's seat also open downwards, allowing the pilot enough room to get in. In the interests of stability, I had to fit the legs with detents or snap-together joints.

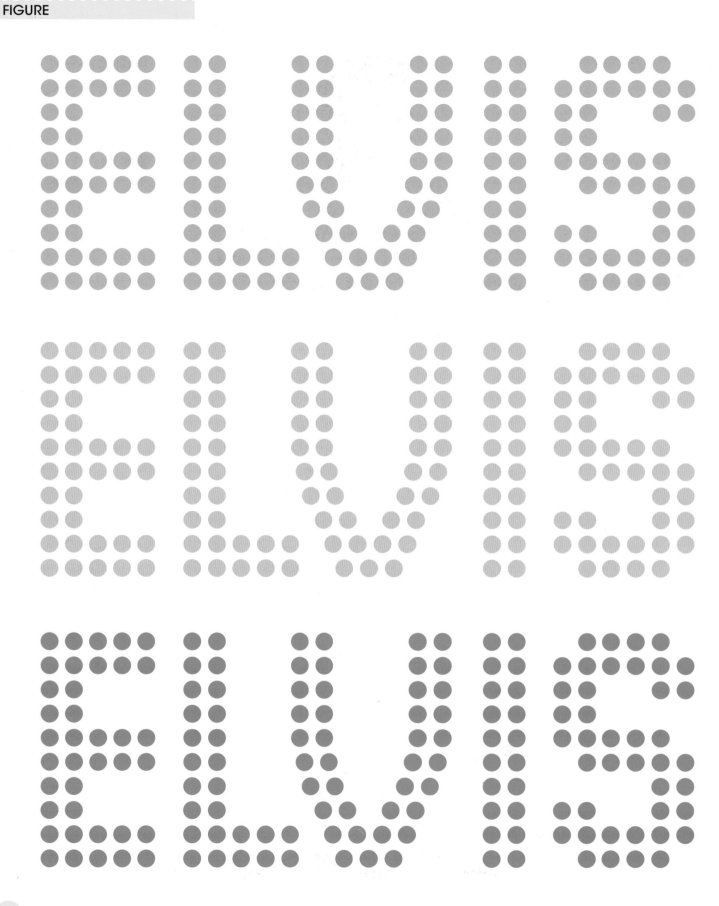

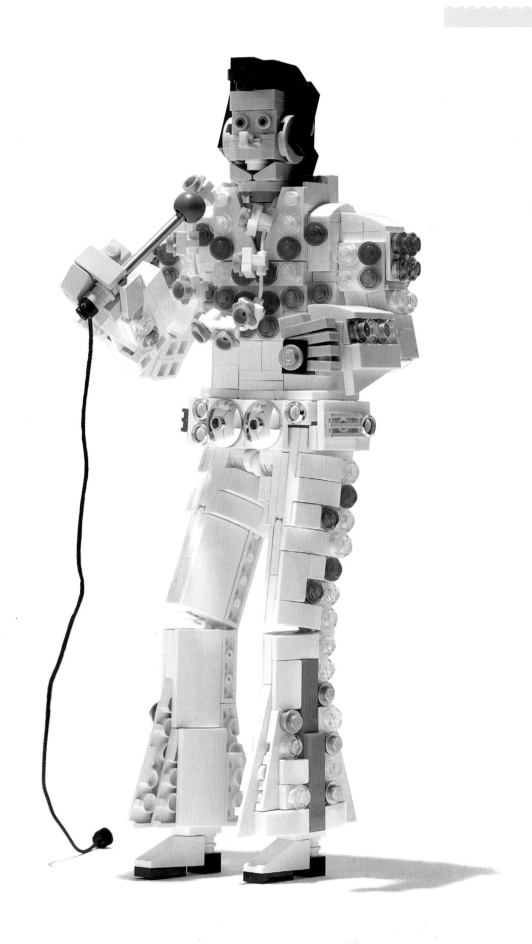

ELVIS

The King lives!

Even though he may have shrunk a little …

It is quite practicable to bring every remotely famous celebrity to life on such a medium scale. There is, of course, the internet example of Freddie Mercury, who was instantly recognizable without too much trouble. We wanted to try this out for ourselves and had a quick think about who else might be easy to recognize. Elvis Presley was the perfect candidate!

In his Hawaii show, he appeared in what was a visually spectacular outfit, and using white bricks, with their wide spectrum of possibilities, we found we could reproduce this brilliantly.

The figure's eyes and nose are a great example of how unlikely parts can be put to good use. The eyes are made from headlight bricks, stuck into flexible hose, cut to length (hose rigid 3 mm, BL: 75).

The nose is made from a hinge element (hinge plate 1x2 locking with one finger on side, BL + LEGO 44567), simply leaving off the counterpart. If the scale of a model allows, such pieces lend themselves perfectly to alternative uses. Often enough, a particularly important element may even dictate the scale of an entire model. It is all always a question of what can be done and what is available.

You can see from Elvis's leg how the direction of the studs can be turned 180°, if the plate is strong enough. Unfortunately, you will need to resort to vintage material for this purpose as LEGO only produced this type of finger hinge (hinge plate 1x2 with three fingers, BL: 4275, and hinge plate 1x2 with two fingers, BL: 4276) until 2006.

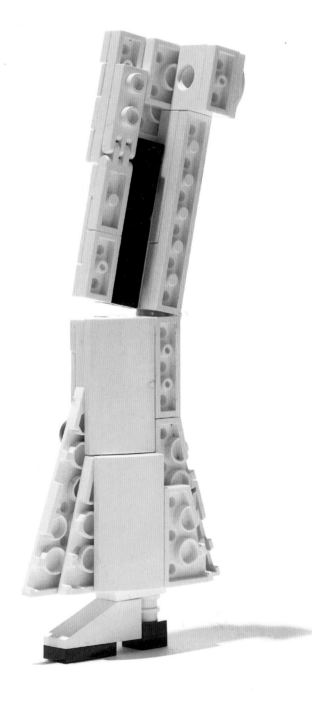

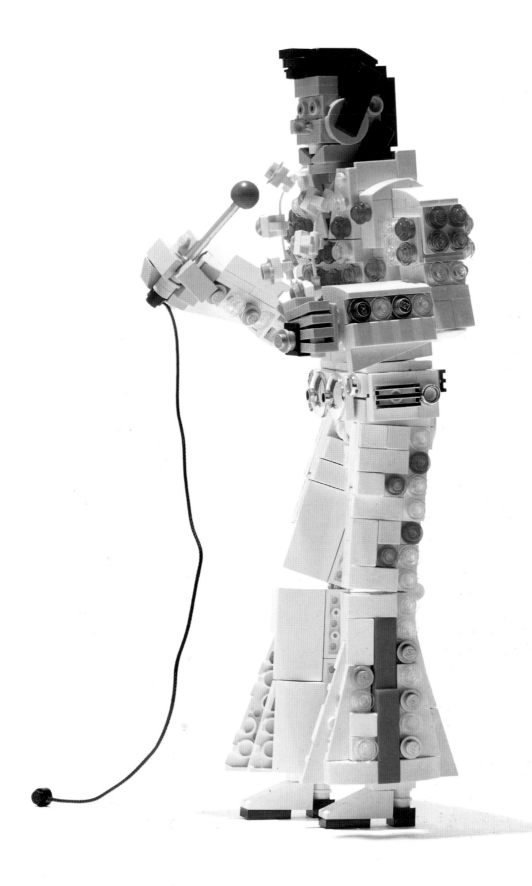

WAINWRIGHT'S WORKSHOP

This half-timbered building, formerly a wainwright's workshop, uses many construction techniques. There are various possible ways of reproducing half-timbering, and the effort involved and the result will be very different, depending on the variation.

The easiest version, which is also the most versatile, is with applied tiles, where the timbers are simply fastened to the wall. This means you can attach many different diagonal beams, as the tiles are fixed to a single stud on the wall and can therefore be turned in any direction you want. The way you use the bricks makes a big difference here. You can build the ordinary 1x1 bricks with studs on the side in the normal way or you can use headlight bricks with a 1x1 plate on top or underneath. Changing the position of the studs gives you many options for arranging the tiles on them. However, at the same time the advantage of this variation results in a rather unrealistic look, as the beams in a half-timbered wall are actually flush with the wall or even a little recessed, instead of standing out.

You can make it even easier for yourself by building the ordinary beams vertically from 1x1 bricks and horizontally from two rows of plates, one on top of the other, and only tiling the diagonal struts as described above.

In the pictures [below] you can see a piece of finished half-timbering as well as one with the studs on the front and one with the undersides of the bricks on the back of the wall.

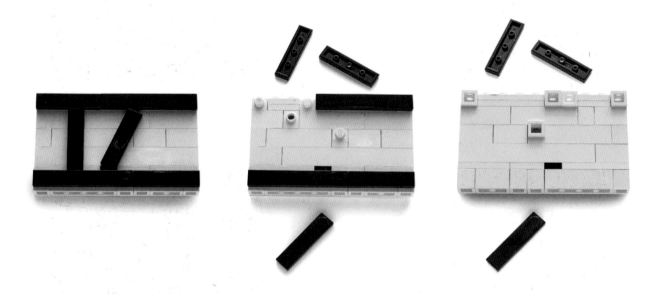

With another option for building timber struts in a wall, the beams lie in the wall. On the one hand, this has the advantage of a realistic appearance, but on the other only one angle is possible. Each time it is determined by the bricks around it—in our two examples below by the 75° slopes and the 30° cheese-graters. In in both cases the beams are simply clamped between the bricks of the wall. In the red brick wall we have used an extra brick at the back to prevent penetration. However, it is not essential to add this extra piece, for example if you want to extend the inner space but it can also be added in the beige-colored wall without any difficulty. The red cheese-graters are held in place by 1x1 bricks with side studs. In this example they are dark red with one black one on the vertical beam.

Once again the pictures [below] show the front and back of the small segments of wall.

For this half-timbered building I decided on the applied tiles version. As the wall color (old light yellow) is only available in a very few shapes, large walls are not possible.

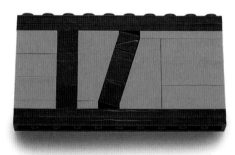

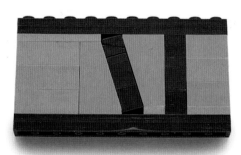

STAIRS AND TURRET

Instead of all the old, destroyed and ruinous elements, here I would like to point out the steps required to construct my half-timbered building. To build such elements there are once again two options: Either you first build an almost complete model and deliberately take parts out later and replace them with smaller or modified parts, such as positive or negative slopes, plates, tiles, etc. or you deliberately build in the holes and destroyed areas straight away. In addition, with these steps, pieces are deliberately not pressed right down, in order to heighten the ruined effect.

As a nice extra, especially for old buildings, you can give the house a little turret. The basis for this is the plate modified 2x2 with bar frame octagonal (BL: + LEGO: 30033). Upright clip plates (plate modified 1x1 with horizontal clip, BL: 6019, LEGO: 61252) are clipped to this and normal plates pressed onto them. As an octagon contains a square, you can join these neatly at the top with a 1x1 brick with five studs and then complete it with a cone on top.

CHIMNEY AND ROOF

There are also several different ways of representing smoke. Elsewhere in this book we show smoke coming from a gun. Here, however, we are talking about the chimney of a house with a little cloud of smoke emerging from it. An easy yet very pretty way of doing this is to pile up a few ice balls.

The soffits along the edges of the two roofs are typical of old houses. This "wooden" version was built from plates, tiles, and hinge plates, and fixed to four studs.

Roofs can also be built of a large number of different parts. Here we wanted to have a version that suited the type of building and we used the very versatile wedges—deliberately upright, so the curves of the wedges give a lovely overall impression of roof tiles. As can be clearly seen in the photo detail [below], here they are used alternately at the normal plate spacing and with extra space created by an additional plate.

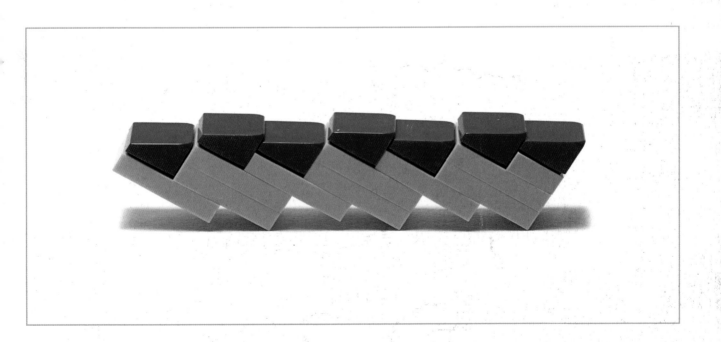

Besides the wedges, another option for making a roof look more rustic is to use 1x2 tiles on long, narrow plates. As, unlike all other tiles and plates, the underside has no bar, these can be placed anywhere on a stud. That means every other row is free from the fixed position that was actually intended and the tiles can half overlap, just like real roof tiles.

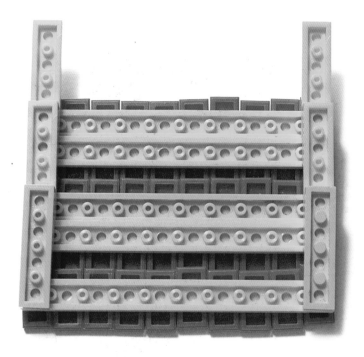

A third, very interesting variation on the roof structure is using ordinary minifigure chairs for a different purpose. Their rounded corners also give the roof the typical shingled look. However, a distance of one stud must be maintained between one row of shingles and the next, but this is no problem with this large size. At the edge of the roof this space will be covered by the soffit so that every second row will not have a hole by the last shingle.

The roof structure is very dense and compact, so sufficient space must be planned in when using this variation. The studs for fixing the soffits can be clearly seen in the picture detail.

DOOR

The supposedly round-arched door in 6W (6 wide, i.e. six studs wide) is actually a rectangular door opening. It only looks round because the edge of the round arch is suggested with tiles. The vertical sides consist of 1x1 bricks with side studs and the horizontal part consists of a vertical 2x8 plate, which has been covered with tiles, jumpers (1x2 tiles with a central stud) and 1x1 plates.

TOWER

A few neat construction techniques can also make a feature of largish pieces of ancient stonework, such as this tower, whose floors can be clearly distinguished when you look more closely.

To convert the window on the bottom floor to these proportions (width of casement approx. 3W), the clear glass panels were simply turned through 90°, as LEGO does not make any windows of this width. To give it the appropriate lead glass look, there is a fence behind the window (fence 1x4x2, BL: + LEGO: 3185), also turned through 90°. The beige-colored wedges finishing the top of the window to look like sandstone are created from brick-colored wedges turned through 180°. As the two together on top of one another have a thickness of 2½ plates, the half plate thickness is evened out by the flat beige-colored brackets (bracket 1x2–2x2, BL: + LEGO: 44728).

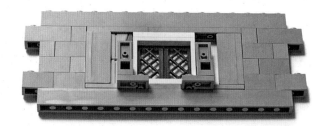

In addition to the construction of the first floor window, the small windows demonstrate yet another way of using the very popular wedges. Positioned vertically, four of them fit neatly into a second opening in the wall and with a second row above them form a nice little window shutter with the X shape that is so typical of my homeland. They are edged with tiles above and below, so that once again the difference in height from the normal bricks is evened out.

In order to be able to apply the central struts of the cross-bar window in this smaller version, we used one of the oldest LEGO building methods in which, back in the early days of LEGO, parts were used a different way round: simply clamping the plate (or, as in this case, the tiles) in between two studs.

For the big windows we also need big shutters. They are constructed in almost exactly the same way as the small ones, though here the larger cheese-grater was used instead of the small wedges. This means it is no longer necessary to even out the difference in height above and below with a row of tiles.

The shutters stand out slightly from the wall, which is intentional, firstly because it is more realistic than an even surface and secondly because one half of the cheese-grater prevents penetration into the interior of the building. The other half can be fixed with a headlamp brick and a tile, as can be clearly seen in the photo detail of the back of the window.

WINTER LANDSCAPE

A wintery landscape always has something calming about it and snow is
also quite easy to reproduce using
white plates. However, here we intend to go into more detail about
the gate, the snowman, and the
sledge that we have shown once but
not explained.

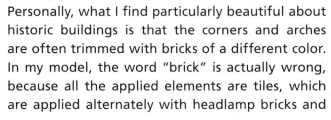

Personally, what I find particularly beautiful about
historic buildings is that the corners and arches
are often trimmed with bricks of a different color.
In my model, the word "brick" is actually wrong,
because all the applied elements are tiles, which
are applied alternately with headlamp bricks and

1x1 bricks with side studs. The photo detail shows
this construction inside the vertical edge of the
gate, though this is identical with the construction
of normal house corners.

The arch then rises almost seamlessly over the edge
above; a single plate under the last stud brick raises
it slightly, so that the row of tiles rises in a slight
curve.

Under the long arch (1x12x3) there are alternating
1x1 bricks with one and two studs arranged with
the upper stud pointing forward. The 1x1 and 1x2
tiles are then pressed on to these alternately, with
some extra 1x2 tiles on the remaining studs of the
1x1 bricks with two studs.

SNOWMAN

For the snowman, the big ball is made from four 2x2 inverted radar dishes around a 1x1 brick with five studs. The inside of the medium ball also consists of a 1x1 brick with five studs. The arms are fixed to its sides. On the front, the vertical clip is positioned in front of the head in such a way that it can hold an orange-colored horn for the nose. Don't forget the hat and broom!

SLEDGE

Just like the rocking chair that we featured in the furniture chapter, this sledge is built with the aid of two whips. Given a slightly different shape, they are used here for runners.

LITTLE AMSTERDAM

We can also demonstrate a few tips and tricks using the example of Little Amsterdam. For instance, the curtains behind the windows of the house on the left are just negative 75° slopes. A great curtain can also be produced in combination with the positive slopes.

We will see the construction of the small tree later with a big tree, but here you can find out how far you can get, if you want to achieve a lot with a small amount of material. These trees were made with just 12 large leaf parts. To make them nevertheless look denser and more voluminous, they are simply added together. One leaf is fixed in a specific place and one (or even two) more are inserted into one another at the broad part. Although this join wobbles, it stays in place, and the wobbling has the happy side effect that the leaves all hang different ways, which here, as with a tree, makes them look more organic.

■DETAILS

Small details add up to produce a consistent overall impression, even if not everything is revealed at
first glance. Here, for example, the combination of
a bicycle tire and the bottom part of a joystick has
produced a quayside that literally speaking neatly
rounds off a harbor scene.

Later, with my sailing ship, we will see this technique
used again to create the upper end of the anchor.

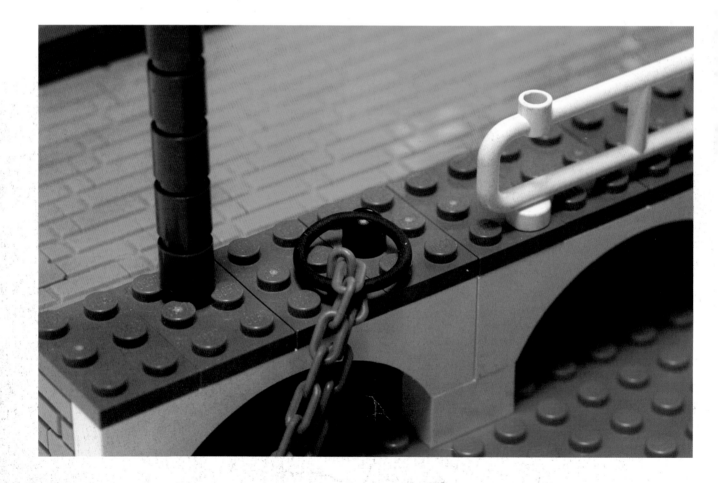

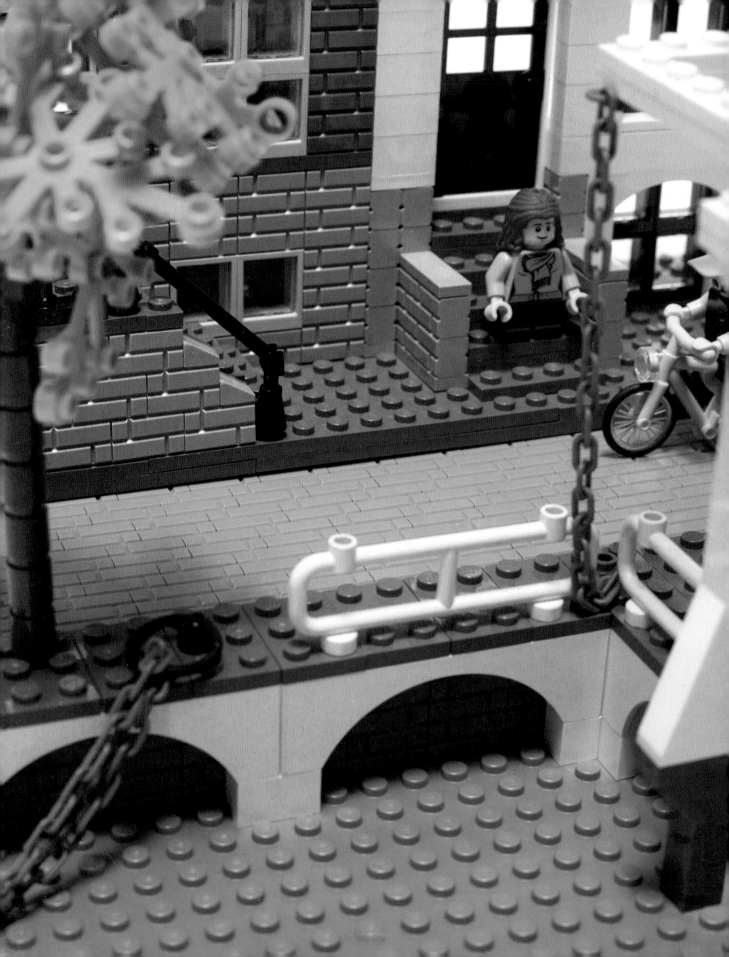

PAVED ROAD

What works on the wall can also work perfectly when laid flat on the ground. Here we have made a paved road from just 1x2 profile bricks, which, in a row, produce a lovely water surface.

When an ordinary brick with a width of 1W is laid on studs, it is exactly the same height as a normally produced brick. Then you lay a plate on top to fix and frame the surface and it immediately results in quite different ground surfaces.

GABLE

For the last detail, it just remains to consider the two gable decorations. It can already be seen from these two variations that a wide range of different-shaped pieces can be used to create these typical house decorations. Arch bricks are particularly obvious and, of course, once again I always enjoy using wedges.

KNIGHT`S CASTLE

Along with historical shipping, my other grand passion is the Middle Ages. And what is closer to that than building huge castles? And of course there are countless opportunities to introduce great tricks into the architecture. Let's begin where the tour of a castle usually starts: at the gate.

You have already learnt about how the gate itself is constructed in the winter landscape.

The cobbled paving consists of round 1x1 plates and 2x2 round plates with rounded bottoms (boat stud), (BL: + LEGO: 2654), which are simply placed between the studs.

This type of paving can also be supplemented with ordinary 2x2 round tiles, 1x1 round tiles, and other round plates, but the round plates with rounded bottoms give the whole thing a harmonious look.

ROUND TOWER

Towers are what castles are all about. There are several basic geometric shapes for castle towers, but the most typical is the round tower. One of the most popular and simplest versions is an alternating pattern of ordinary bricks (usually 1x2 bricks) and 1x1 round bricks. Using round bricks allows the wall to curve in almost any radius you want. With 1x2 bricks the smallest possible diameter is about 10 cm.

Where it widens out at the battlements, the quarter-circle bricks were used negatively and the two opposite studs were tiled.

The wall up by the battlements is twice as thick, so here we simply put two circular walls of different diameter together.

Here I would like to take the opportunity to show you a variation of circular building on a completely different model. A curve can also be built using 1x2 round plates and 1x1 plates alternately. What's more, you can allow free rein to your imagination. When I had seen Phil's tower, I quickly built this surfer's wave overnight. From the side view you can also get a good look at the positioning of the foam.

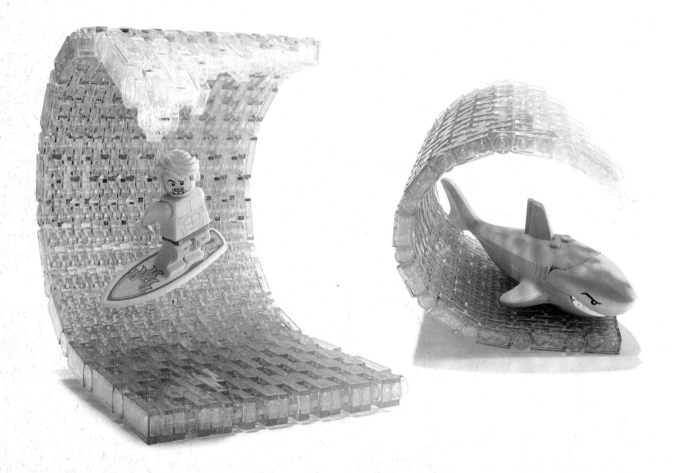

KEEP AND WINDOWS

The keep (the tallest tower of the castle) can also be built using the round technique. As LEGO has had round tiles in its range for a number of years, the individual circular walls can now be finished off with a row of tiles, and then a further, very slightly smaller circular wall can be placed on it, thus tapering the tower as it goes up.

The two windows in the gable wall to the right of the tower are exactly like the door of the half-timbered house: only round-arched at first glance. Here too the impression is achieved through the arrangement of the applied tiles. As with the large windows in the tower, the actual glass element is constructed using fences and backed with rectangular yellow transparent 1x1 plates to close the gaps in the fence. The arrangement of the headlamp and SNOT bricks can be clearly seen in the photo detail.

FAÇADE

Another typical basic shape for a tower is the octagon. When you build the walls above the brick hinges, gaps appear at the corners. These can be attractively filled with wedges and tiles, each alternately bridging to headlamp bricks. This trick of breaking up the visual outline allows the same thing to happen at 45° corners.

There are also many different ways of using rock bricks. Personally, I always like it when this kind of rock face has corners and edges that flow smoothly into one another. That is why I have covered every possible stud appearing in the wall with the next row of slopes, a tuft of grass, or something similar. The cross-shaped windows fit brilliantly into the medieval theme. If you look carefully, you will notice that they consist of the legs of minifigures, which can be pulled away from the hip joints if you use a little force. After that the two lower legs are placed upright, foot to foot, and the upper pair are fixed to stud bricks and above the rear sitting position hole in the legs.

ROOF AND DORMER

Soffits, the finishing strips of a roof, are typical of historic buildings. Unlike the roof of the half-timbered house, the roof of my castle is made of ordinary roof tiles. There is not enough space on the small gable of the dormer window to attach ordinary SNOT bricks or angle plates, so simple versions of clamping are used here to join the dormer window to the soffit. The clip of a horizontal clip plate is simply pushed in between the angle rod (plate modified 1x2 with arm up (horizontal arm length 5 mm), BL: + LEGO: 88072) and the roof tiles.

WELL

One thing the inner courtyard of the castle must
have is a well. This one has an extra roof with
shingles made from black minifigure fins. Either
you press individual fins row by row on the underside of a large black plate or, as here in the picture,
at various heights on thin supporting strips.
The circular wall consists almost entirely of jumpers
(1x2 plates with a single stud) and the top row is
made of tiles.

ARROW SLITS

Arrow slits are, of course, also essential; they are an important element of every defensive wall. The realistic construction of such slits is broad on the inside and narrow on the outside. This provided the crossbow archers with plenty of room, while they themselves were well-protected. Wedges are ideal here too. However, in order to get them to form a smooth surface and lie flush with one another, you have to build them in as shown in the photo detail.

SPIRE

Building a roof on a round or polygonal base is always a challenge. In this case the base is octagonal and the lower part also flares out. For this reason there was no question of using the construction technique shown in the half-timbered house here, so another solution had to be found. The LEGO angle plate with the sharpest angle (wedge plate 12x3) is also too blunt for this task. So we needed a special construction here that had the flattened part at the bottom and could offer a suitable ratio between length and breadth. The solution was provided by eight triangles made up of plates and tiles meeting one another at the top and secured at the bottom with an extra brick to prevent slipping. That is how you close the cap. Finally the whole construction was fastened together with two Technic rubber bands.

■DETAILS

In this picture we also want to show you the sub-structure of a model. This is a wonderful way of using up unwanted colors, old or damaged bricks, or large, superfluous pieces to form a stable base. The 1x8x2 arch built into the wall is another example of rounded arches using headlamp bricks with tiles. Similarly, for doors or gateways the vertical sides would then only need tiles on stud bricks for everything to look right.

Because it belongs here, we'd like to show you the weathervane again at this point, the one you have already seen once right at the beginning of this book. It's a lovely detail, made almost entirely by combining parts in a different way from their original purpose: the direction indicators are small hammers, the rooster's tail is a hat feather and the beak is a hand.

DECIDUOUS TREE

The tree chapter is very complex. Just as in real life no single tree is the same as another, so it is in the world of LEGO. I would like to start with a massive example, a deciduous tree with a thick trunk, like a cherry, a chestnut or similar.

The base is the thick trunk, which should of course be round or at least have a round cross-section. This can only be achieved using a single type of brick, the palisade brick (brick modified 1x2 log, BL: + LEGO: 30136).

Because of its rounded outer surfaces it can be arranged that nine bricks make a circle. The grooves and gaps enhance the visual impression of tree bark. At the bottom, the beginnings of the roots are modeled using simple roof tiles and at the top you can exchange the 1x2 bricks for a 1x4 brick in places from where the branches will spring.

And what worked with the small tree in Little Amsterdam will work even better here. This tree looks much fuller because of all the criss-crossing leaves.

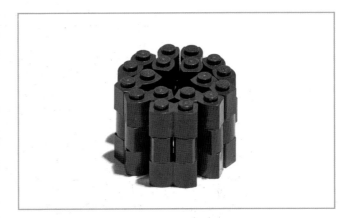

FLOWER-PETAL TREE

This tree also looks like a tree, but when you look at it closely, it is actually a collection of flower petals (plant flower stem 1 x 1 x 2/3 with three large leaves, BL: + LEGO: 6255).

To show more precisely how the fastening works, we have built a simpler version. As can be seen in this picture, the petals are all pressed in place around a five-stud unit. Unfortunately, this construction is rather unstable, as the petals don't grip the studs as well as other pieces. You can fasten as many of these bunches of leaves as you like to the trunk and the branches, depending on how big the tree is to be.

WEEPING WILLOW

Another deciduous tree is the weeping willow. It is made from a combination of ordinary 5x6 leaves and sea grass (plant sea grass, BL: + LEGO: 30093). The sea grass is easily inserted into the holes of the leaves by the pin at the end, 2–4 times per leaf. As with the flower-petal tree, the leaf is then mounted on a branch or directly on to the trunk.

PINE

The pine is intended to show that a tree trunk can also be made entirely without ordinary bricks–well, almost, at least. You start with as many 1x1 cones as you like (preferably about four). Then you simply thread flexible cables (hose rigid 3 mm BL: 75) through their hollow studs and twist them together. To make the construction more stable you can pull a Technic rubber band around the flexible hose as well. Then at the upper end you just insert the hoses into the hollow studs of the leaves. More leaves are then attached to the basic leaves to complete the crown of the tree.

BUSHES

These two bushes are just made from two different parts. Three pairs of sword leaves (plant leaves 6x5 swordleaf with clip, BL: + LEGO: 10884) are placed back to back and bound together either with a Technic rubber band (BL: x88 black, LEGO: 4107153) or with a short band with studs at the end (BL: x127c11 black, LEGO: 4109714). Then comes a second row of leaves, which is pressed on to the studded underside of the first row. If you like, you can stabilize the bush by assembling a row of round 1x1 bricks and pressing it into the middle of the leaves.
This method of construction is also applicable to coniferous trees.

SWORD-LEAVE FIR

The construction of the first fir tree we want to demonstrate here is based on the bush we have just shown. The entire fir tree is made up of sword leaves with a conical trunk running up to them. The vertical stems that are increasingly angled toward the center will later give the fir tree its natural shape – from the broad part directly above the ground to the thin tip. As can be seen in the picture, one possible way of making it is to use 1x1 bricks with a vertical handle at the bottom and above them the brown 2x2 round plates with four arms up, which were specially designed by LEGO for trees and fixing leaves. After that come the already ageing palm tops, which are also made from plates with four arms up but closer to the center. The leaves are then clipped by their pegs to all these handles and arms, and rotated around the stems as desired until everything fits.

LONG-TRUNK FIR

With this fir tree the foliage sits on a long trunk. This version is only intended to show the different types and variations, which are, after all, quite natural. The foliage could equally well sit directly on the ground or be set up on the fir tree shown previously.

The difference between this fir tree and the previous one lies in the way the trunk is built. Here the leaves are clipped to 2x4 bricks, which in turn are mounted on various clips: at the bottom on long, thick round-ended clips (which have infinitely variable rotation, because of the rounded stud at the end), above that to ordinary vertical clips in a 2x2 arrangement (each in a different direction), and lastly once again the vertical clips on top of one another, rotated through 90° each time. The crown of the fir is then finished off with a bush, as already described.

Once again the trunk consists of 1x2 palisade bricks, as for the large deciduous tree, but here quite normally two side by side in each row, then rotated through 90° in the next row. The whole construction can be broken up by occasionally replacing a palisade brick with a round, brown 1x1 brick or three-leaf units (plant brick, round 1x1 with three bamboo leaves, BL: + LEGO: 30176) or simply two three-leaf units.

PALM-LEAVE FIR

This fir tree starts at the bottom in almost the same way as the previous one, with a long trunk of 1x2 palisade bricks. However, with this tree lianas are wound around the trunk. The interesting thing is that this is not actually a proper part but only the fixture holding a part, the three-petal flower. When you have removed the flower from the holder, these bits are left over as waste. But what is to prevent us from snipping them off with a pair of scissors and building them into our decoration? In this case we have fixed the ends of a few of these pieces to our tree: on branches, other lianas, cone units etc., thus creating a kind of liana or creeper.

For the foliage of this fir tree we actually do use leaves, large and small palm leaves to be precise. In order to represent the way it tapers, we start at the bottom with four large leaves (attach them all by the last stud on the 2x2 trunk at the angle of your choice). Repeat the entire process one to three times. Next come the large leaves, but now two at a time, turned through 180° and each attached by both studs to the 2x2 base. Then two more leaves, but turned through 90. Then repeat the entire process once more, but this time with the small palm leaves.

To avoid having too abrupt a transition to the top, build in a further two or three rows of three-leaf units and top it all off with a small original fir tree.

FIR

Although the two long fir-tree trunks look nice, they are unfortunately a bit unstable, so here we show a more stable version. The base is formed of the flexible hose, which we have often mentioned before. It starts in a 2x2 round brick (as this has an axle hole) and runs up inside the trunk as far as the foliage. In between you can insert as many 1x1 bricks with five studs alternating with round 1x1 bricks as you like. Press 1x2 tiles on to the studs, turning them all at different angles. Although the trunk has a tendency to bend a little, it remains stable because of the flexible cable inside.

FIR TREE FROM PLATES

This last fir is intended to demonstrate that you can even make small fir trees without any special leaf elements. It consists entirely of an assemblage of plates that get shorter and shorter as they go up. Fastened in different directions on individual studs they produce an overall image of a cone. It just needs a trunk, then the simple tree is finished.

FIR TREE FROM LEAVES

Again, this fir tree consists only of a trunk and leaf elements piled on top of one another. However, as you near the top the leaves must be turned through 90° and attached vertically, to form a point.

WATER

Water can be reproduced in a number of different ways. Four of them are presented in detail here.

The first version is very plain, but also allows the parts below the surface of the water to be seen. All you need is transparent base plates, which are framed at the sides by the structure of the shore.

For the second version you simply press transparent light blue 1x2 tiles on the transparent base plates. As can be seen in the picture, you can make the plain water a little more interesting in many different ways, such as using water-lily leaves made from ordinary green 2x2 round plates.

As a third variation, any surface (but preferably keeping to blue) can be scattered with transparent 1x1 round plates, preferably transparent light blue combined with clear and a few ordinary white ones to represent foam. The loose scattering ensures a realistic surface that reflects the light in all directions. The water for my sailing ship was represented in the same way.

The fourth and final option utilizes a completely blue "wall" built horizontally. In order to make the plain blue surface a bit prettier you can use white plates to suggest waves and currents. In addition foam, rocks, and other items can be placed on it using headlamp bricks. Objects can also be integrated into the surface. The water lilies are again made from the three-petal flowers. You just have to leave a suitable gap in the blue wall so that you can insert the petals.

THE GALLEON *REVENGE*

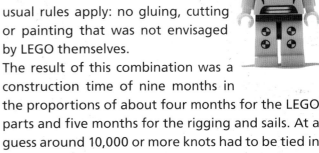

The following model, a 1:50 scale reproduction of the galleon "Revenge" of 1577—Sir Francis Drake's flagship in the war against the Spanish Armada—, is my own most beautiful, most demanding and most difficult model.

All the same, in this case I have to make an exception to the rule of working **exclusively** with LEGO. When constructing reproductions of historic ships the LEGO options for rigging and sails are rather too limited, so it is better to change over to ordinary building materials. However, apart from that, all the usual rules apply: no gluing, cutting or painting that was not envisaged by LEGO themselves.

The result of this combination was a construction time of nine months in the proportions of about four months for the LEGO parts and five months for the rigging and sails. At a guess around 10,000 or more knots had to be tied in order to put all the sails in place correctly.

HULL

The biggest challenge was definitely the hull, which has a unique construction method. Its special feature is that it is curved along three axes. As LEGO is almost exclusively based on right angles, this rule will be broken first.

The planks of the hull consist of long rows of 1x4 tiles and 1x4 plates, joined so they are staggered by two studs. The adjacent model of a small boat, which was made as an extra to show the technique used for the planking (in the Revenge this part is no longer visible), was built using two 1x2 plates each time instead of a 1x4 plate, to produce a curve with a smaller radius.

When several of these long planks are lined up next to each other and joined in places at the back with 1x2 plates, they can be curved along two axes. The third curved axis was achieved by fastening individ-ual planks or small groups of planks in the middle of the ship to pivot mountings, which enabled any angle to be infinitely varied while at the same time holding the planks in place.

All the same, what don't turn out so well with this technique are the lower edges of the planking. As these are curved and the outer ones don't run the whole length of the ship, they have to end somewhere at the bottom edge. This results in a stepped edge, but this can be cleverly covered by many thousands of small, light blue, transparent 1x1 round plates. As a ship actually looks much better in direct contact with the water, the problem of the rough lower edge leads to a logical and attractive solution. At the stern, the planks then run straight, ending at the transom (the back wall of the ship). At the front, they end near the bow, as this curve would have too small a radius. The bow is then built from separate round elements and closes the gap between the sides and the bowsprit (the central spar at the front of the ship).

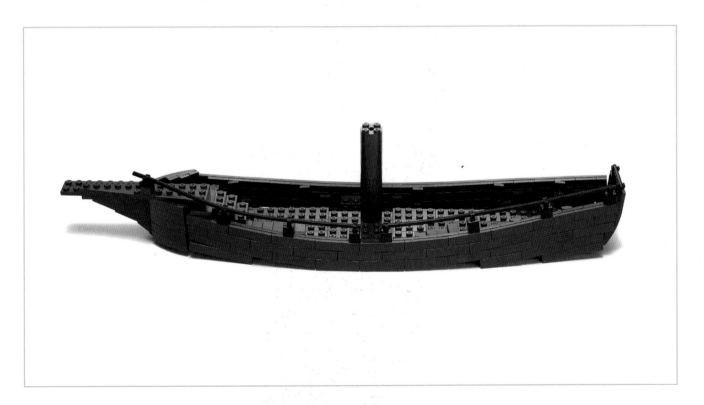

CROW'S NEST

Above the mainstays (the rigging), on each of the big masts there is a crow's nest. As these were round on the Revenge, the use of a large, brown cartwheel (wheel wagon giant, 56 mm D., BL: + LEGO: 33212) suggested itself. The advantage of this version is the strength of the outer rim, because all kinds of clip connections can be cleverly attached to it.

▐ LADDER

The ladder for climbing up to the poop deck (highest and sternmost deck) is assembled on the same principle as the castle window: the tiles are simply clamped between the plates. Simple, but absolutely perfect in this situation.

FIRE AT WILL

In order to represent Lego in motion, i.e. "control the action," fleeting elements such as smoke, explosions, flying pieces of debris etc. are reproduced as snapshots. In this case it's cannonballs and slingshots in flight, both of which are a must for every adventure-loving child. For these two examples we need an ordinary round shot and a chain shot (which was specially designed to destroy the enemy rigging). In pictures containing movement, we very often work with transparent material to fix pieces flying through the air as invisibly as possible. In the two preceding pictures the smoke for both shots is represented first and then, at a distance, created by the transparent bricks, the cannonballs. The smoke will also be a different shape, depending on the position of the cannonball.

CANNONS AND SWIVEL GUN

There are a few LEGO pieces that enjoy a certain popularity with model-builders, usually because they are small, versatile, and can be used flexibly. These of course include the wedges we have mentioned many times before, and also the Pneumatic T Pieces (new style, T bar, BL: + LEGO: 4697b). These pieces form the rear axle for the left and right cannons and at the same time the elevation mechanism for the barrel.

The T Piece also forms the basis of the swivel gun (the small hand-fired cannon on the railing). It was extended with short pieces of rubber pneumatic hose and completed at the back with gear shift levers.

LANTERN

The lantern at the upper end of the transom is very simply constructed and essentially consists of just two different sized radar dishes (dish 2x2 inverted (radar), BL: + LEGO: 4740; dish 3x3 inverted (radar), BL: + LEGO: 43898), four lattice windows (window 1 x 2 x 2 2/3 pane lattice diamond with rounded top, BL: + LEGO: 30046) and an ordinary rod in 4L (length 4). First the rod is inserted in the 3x3 radar dish with the curve outwards. The small 2x2 radar dish is mounted on it in the opposite direction and then pushed fully into the 3x3 dish.

In the center of the lantern, a yellow transparent 1x1 round brick can now be threaded on to the rod. The two different radar dishes, one inside the other, are mounted again on the other end of the rod but this time facing in the other direction. The four lattice windows can now be carefully inserted vertically in between and finally clamped in place by pushing the radar dishes together.

DINGHY

Although LEGO produces small ready-made boats, I wanted something bigger and, in particular, something I had made myself. So on a very plain surface of vertical SNOT tiles and plates I placed a rounded bow element. Here, as in the big ship, the curved pieces used (slope, curved 4x1, no studs, BL: + LEGO: 61678) form the bow. However, the problem in this instance is the openly visible back of the construction.

I managed to make a very narrow, inconspicuous connection here with vertical clip plates, a short clip rod, and a short piece of pneumatic hose. The most important aspect of this was that the rubbery surface of the hose enabled the short rod of the clip to be clamped in place.

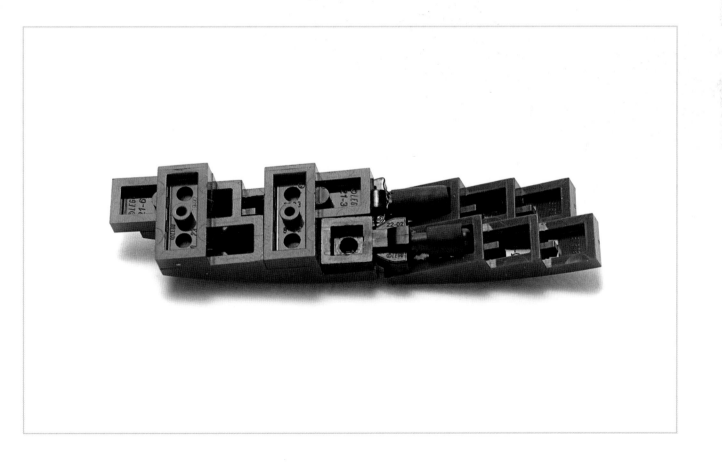

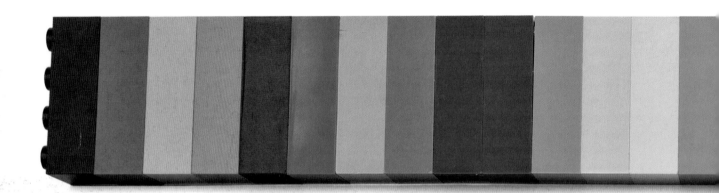

A TRIP TO THE COLOR MUSEUM

On the following pages we will devote ourselves to the many colors in existence and their names. As a framework we have come up with the idea of a museum, in which the colors are presented in the form of exhibits. This is followed by a summary in table form of the names of colors with the usual definition of the color and also LEGO's own color names. We have taken the trouble to build some monochrome models in each color. This means you can discover further construction techniques and NPUs. And every now and then there are explanations of construction methods, special features etc.

STATUES

In the entrance area there are already a few statues that cleverly unite construction techniques and NPUs. On the following pages you can take a closer look at the individual figures, all built in **white**.

Kneeling cupid: For the "bent" leg you can put a single minifigure leg in front of the figure. The other leg is built from plates and roof tiles. A cow horn with the small lever (see the front of the book) simulates the bow and arrow. The white hair is a rarity; it was only available in this color 1975–82. On the other hand, the wings are from the current Chima Series.

Scribe: This scribe can hold the tablet because the hand fits into the round opening at the back.

Javelin thrower: The javelin is made from a white lightsaber handle.

Pharaoh: If you do not have a complete white head available, you could, for instance, turn a skeleton to face backwards, as in the case of this pharaoh.

Stonemason: The beard is made of softer material, which allows it to be "stressed," by which we mean putting a little too much strain on an element, as here, for example, when we push the beard a little to the right, so it fits in with the stiff hair.

Scholar: The end of this staff is made of the globe: finial round, raised (Scala Roof, Belville Bed) BL: x12, LEGO: 4249742.

Discus thrower: This hair is a Q-part, but can be found at BrickLink (no. 3901).

Tuareg: While I was building I kept getting more ideas for monochrome figures. This Tuareg's sword is called minifig, weapon sword, scimitar.

Hippocrates: Here a Clikits pin is used to represent the pouch. (It's hard to believe, but I can't find a number for it. These things happen sometimes.)

Justice: The statue of Justice combines several of our favorite elements:
Clikits pins, rubber, and lever bases.

Knight in armor: This knight has a very unusual winged visor, which probably only older LEGO fans will recognize from their youth: minifig, visor old with grille and feather, BL: X105. These visors were available only in the years 1978–84 in the colors black, light gray, and red.

Coachbuilder: This coach wheel in white is available as no. BL: 2470.

■ STOREROOM

New exhibits first of all arrive in the museum storeroom. In this snapshot most colors can actually be found in one go:

Very Light Gray: The camcorder is on the right, on the lid of the table display case at the back. It's a Scala Utensil with the no. BL: 33270.

Very Light Bluish Gray: In this unusual color we show a cat. It's the middle one of the three.

Very Light Orange: This is the cat on the right with the stripe along its back. Officially, this is the only element available in this color. The cat on the left is in Medium Dark Flesh, but we will show this color again on a different exhibit.

Rust: Officially there are only ten pieces in this shade. We show a pennant on a lance to the left behind the automobile. There you can also clearly see the difference from Red.

Light Salmon: A typical Scala color from the 1990s. The faucets in this shade are standing on a tray of the same color on the shelves behind the camcorder.

Brown: This color, which we call "old brown," has not been produced since around 2002. It was replaced by Reddish Brown. The monochrome Mongol is standing on the right next to the cactus.

Dark Flesh: Look at the head of the gentleman wearing the hat. So far it has only been used for two security guards from two Superhero series. Another head in this color appears on the ambulance driver in the Spiderman Set 4857.

Fabuland Orange: As the name tells us, this color appeared only in Fabuland. Here we show a luggage cart.

Bright Light Yellow: The pretty assistant's hairdo.

Light Lime: Another color not often used. The 1x1 tiles with clip on the second shelf also show how the SNOT technique can be used to steer negative building in two directions.

The Martian's head and arms are **Medium Green**; his legs are **Purple**.

Sand Green: In this case we'll just say "cactus."

The garish lantern at the entrance is unmistakably in **Light Turquoise**.

Aqua: BURP stands for Big Ugly Rock Piece. Here the color is marbled with White.

Yellowish Green: Look for the bionicle mask on the shelves.
Sky Blue: Look for the tile with the white cross and you will also see this color.
Dark Blue-Violet: A Roman twin combination, made of four 1x4 plates. Right next to the helmet in **Chrome Blue**.

For their break, the two museum employees have placed a milk carton (BL: 33011a) and a jar of jelly (BL: 33011c) in **Light Violet** on the table.

Medium Lavender: An inflatable dolphin.

In the middle of the picture are two flowers, the lower one in **Medium Dark Pink** and the upper one in **Pink**.

In the Clikits series there are a large number of exclusive transparent colors. We didn't manage to get hold of **Trans-Light Purple** before the photo shoot. That's why you will find **Trans-Pink** and **Trans-Very Light Blue** in front of the milk carton.

You don't very often see a treasure chest in **Trans-Dark Pink** either.

Chrome Antique Brass: In the open display case is a key in this color. Here you can also find the little crown in **Chrome Pink** and the small Rock in **Chrome Green**. The sword in **Flat Dark Gold** can also be easily distinguished from the others.

Between the shelves is a fender in **Metallic Green** (BL: 32189).

There are also luminescent colors that glow in the dark after absorbing light. **Glow in the Dark White** is one of these three colors. Look in the chest for Reddish Brown, where there are a few bars in 4L (4 studs long). The second is **Glow in the Dark Opaque**, represented by the knives that were used as teeth for the snake in Harry Potter.

And there are also glitter colors: **Glitter Trans-Clear** can be found at the very top on the right (brick, modified 2x24 with peg at each end, BL: 47122) and the roof on the far left is in **Glitter Trans-Dark Pink**.

▍SEAHORSE

Trans-Bright Green: At first glance it doesn't look like LEGO, but this seahorse (BL: 51164) has a 2x4 connection and is a large piece of the nicer kind. (It isn't at all aggressive either …)

▍BULLI-SCOUT-WALKER

Light Bluish Gray: With this shade you can use a simple rule. As with Dark Bluish Gray, wedges only come in the bluish shades of gray. The Bulli-Scout-Walker you can see on the next double page, ended up on my to-do list when I saw an AT-AT with the body of a VW bus.

For three years I have also been including at least one head brick per book. This one also pays homage by representing **Black**.

Incidentally, Rajesh Ramayan „Raj" Koothrappali, who is marching across the front of the picture, is wearing a jacket in **Dark Purple**.

What's more, our reference flap tags, which are made up with Droid arms, are always **Dark Orange**.

ELEPHANTS

These elephants come from a LEGO period when only the old shades of gray were available. Accordingly they are **Light Gray** and **Dark Gray**. They are making a stop at a waterhole in **Trans-Light Blue**. A few NPU constructions can also be seen in this diorama; just have a closer look.

SCREWDRIVER

Life-size tools are also popular items to make from our favorite material. The handle of the screwdriver is **Dark Bluish Gray**, and is assembled from wheel rims. The rim pieces are joined inside with Technic axles. The metallic silver pipes are Technic pin connectors round 2L without slot (pin joiner round, BL: 75535). The floor is made of 1x6 tiles in **Dark Tan**.

The newspaper should be included as part of "control the action," because the pages aren't joined together. The museum attendant has a tile in each hand.

AUTOMOBILE SCULPTURE

Owners of the book "Build Your Own LEGO Vehicles" already know this automobile sculpture. It has tires in **Milky White** and stands on a platform in **Dark Red**. Opposite are seats in **Fabuland Brown**.

AUTHOR CONFERENCE

At first glance this is a really nondescript photo. Yet there are a few interesting features, techniques, and colors to be found in the midst of this cheerful authors' conference. The monitor, for example, is once again a 2x2 hinge brick (hinge brick 2x2 top plate thin, BL: 6134). The plastic beakers are represented by unusual pin-joiner-halves (Technic hub/handle 1x1, BL: 424). The table lamps have a barbell weight for their base (minifig, utensil barbell weight, BL: 91049, LEGO: 6092258).

Making the phone booth in **Red** is a time-consuming SNOT task. Can you manage it without instructions? In addition we find the colors **Light Green** in a flower pot and **Trans-Black** as a bottle.

MODERN ART

Yes, the Rock 'n' Roll Wrestling Bashers also go into the museum. The middle one wears a necklace in **Light Pink** (Scala, clothes necklace, BL: x11). The work of art they are gawping at is in **Metallic Silver**. The construction with clips (bar 1L with clip mechanical claw, BL: 48729) means it can be twisted into all possible shapes.

The colorful creations on the high pillar are ice balls in **Salmon** and **Dark Azure**. The treetops by the way present the color **medium lime**.

STAR WARS FIGURES

In the next room of our art gallery we come across a whole series of special colors that appear nearly only in Star Wars. From left to right:

Chrome Black: Darth Vader
Metal Blue: Super Battle Droid
Sand Red: Battle Droid
Chrome Gold: C-3PO
Pearl Light Gold: C-3PO

In the adjoining room is the exclusive key tag in **Chrome Red** on a **Light Orange** base.

DŌMO-KUN

The Superstar Dōmo-kun, famous mainly in Japan, is built in **Reddish Brown**. In order to be able to oppose the teeth, we again used the articulated tube trick, as described for the minions.

The half pin-joiner (Technic hub/handle 1x1, BL: 424) is also used again here as a camera lens.
And how do you like our version of a Mondrian painting?

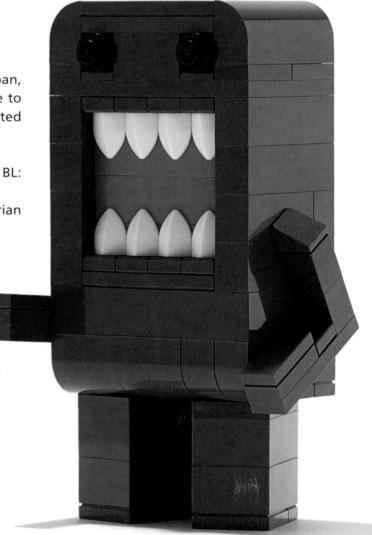

MAMMOTH

Dark Brown: Mammoth

All the attendants in this museum have **Dark Blue** pants and caps and **Medium Blue** shirts.

The light blue bicycle that can be glimpsed through the window in the background has the color name **Medium Azure**.

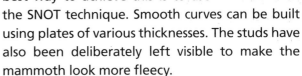

Even though most bricks are rectangular, they are very good for building living creatures. However, you have to take care that the model doesn't become too angular. The best way to achieve this is to use the SNOT technique. Smooth curves can be built using plates of various thicknesses. The studs have also been deliberately left visible to make the mammoth look more fleecy.

For the tusks I used horns (dinosaur tail end section, BL: 40379) and horn extensions (dinosaur tail/neck middle section with pin, BL: 40378). The angle of the trunk was achieved by using a neck bracket (minifig, neck bracket with back stud, BL: 42446).

To make the water with the mammoth's ice floe floating on it look more interesting, under the transparent blue tiles (tile 1x2 with groove, BL: 3069b in **Trans-Dark Blue**) I used plates of different colors, in this case white (BL: white) and light gray (BL: light bluish gray).However, there are plenty of other suitable colors such as dark gray, black, and brown. Just experiment!

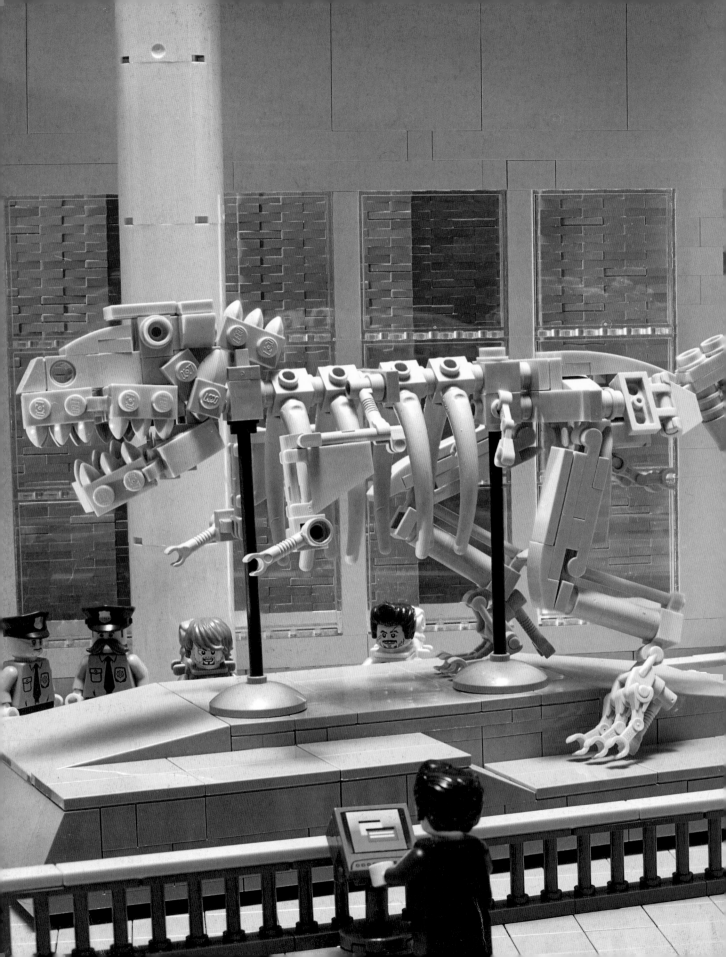

TYRANNOSAURUS REX

Tan: Tyrannosaurus rex. For this exhibit I took the Tyrannosaurus rex in the Field Museum of Natural History in Chicago (USA) as my model. Not exactly a construction involving a "quick build". Here I really had to delve into the rarities box in order to be able to build some sections, so there are a few Q-parts involved. However, this piece of work clearly shows how much you can do with clips. In addition, I had a lot of Droid arms, some of them interlaced. The acute angles can be achieved by attaching plates together with clips. You can see this very well in the teeth.

Once again, the frame is produced from adapted tubes, which are fastened to the saurian at the top with 1x1 round plates with holes (with open stud, BL: 85861, LEGO 6100627).

And in the last picture of the T rex series you can see why parents often wish for a place where they can temporarily leave their children …

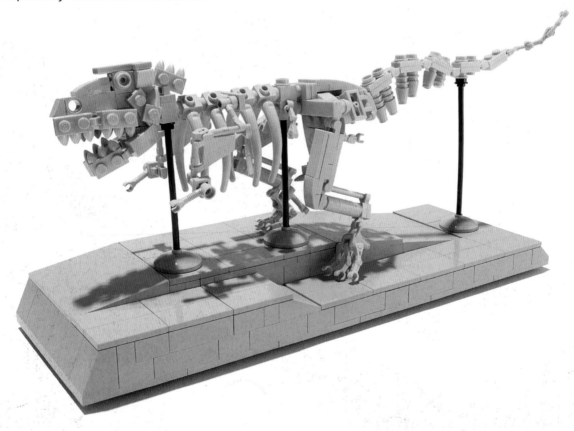

AFTER-SCHOOL CARE

While we're on the subject of after-school care, it is of course also available in our museum. Stocked up with plenty of provisions, the little rascals can enjoy romping about here, no matter whether it's with an ice cream cone in **Medium Orange**, a popsicle in **Trans-Neon Yellow**, or **Trans-Medium Blue** or sausages in **Flesh**.

The animals in this area are very robust: the tiger in **Earth Orange**, the dinosaur in **Bright Green**, or the bear from Toy Story in **Magenta**. So are the **Light Purple** lizard and the snail shell in **Dark Pink**.

What's more, the dragon has **Trans-Neon Orange** wings and a **Chrome Gold** head.

The little **Bright Light Blue** dress comes from the Simpsons series and is usually worn by Maggie (BL: sim005).

■ JANITOR'S OFFICE

Of course, every building of this size has its own janitor. One of them is just having his lunch break with a sausage sandwich in **Light Flesh**. The other two in their **Lime** vests will join him when they have removed the neat black bin bags (black mini-fig, utensil sack/bag with handle, BL: 10169, LEGO 6116487).

A Duplo brick (BL: 3011pb05) in **Dark Yellow** is one of just three elements in this color. However, we can't tell what distinguishes this color from Bright Light Yellow, even when we look closely. Absolutely identical.

At the back on the left you can spot a cart belonging to the cleaning crew. The color I have used for the paper dispenser is called **Light Aqua**. A spring symbolizes paper that has been half pulled out.

The flowerpots also come in many unusual colors, even including **Violet**.

The front tires of the delivery bicycle are inserted in the holes of faucets (tap 1x1, BL: 4599).

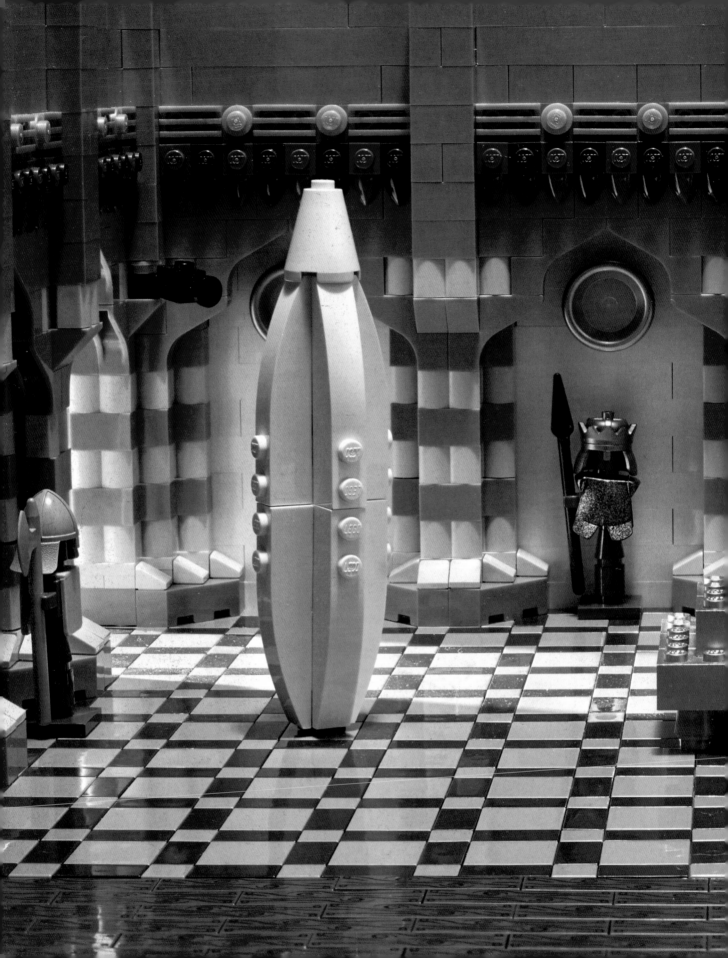

▌ARMORY

This exhibition room displays armor and weapons in these colors:

Medium Dark Flesh:	walls
Light Yellow:	obelisk
Pearl Light Gray:	lance on right
Pearl Dark Gray:	lance on left
Pearl Gold:	sarcophagus
Metallic Gold:	pyramids
Speckle Black-Gold:	Atlantis armor
Speckle Black-Copper:	breastplate

▌PENCIL

The **Orange** pencil is also one of the things we have modeled life size on a scale of 1:1.

The Technic pin connectors round 2L without slot (pin joiner round, BL: 75535) are joined with Technic pins.

The eraser is built with the hinge plate you already know from the Minions.

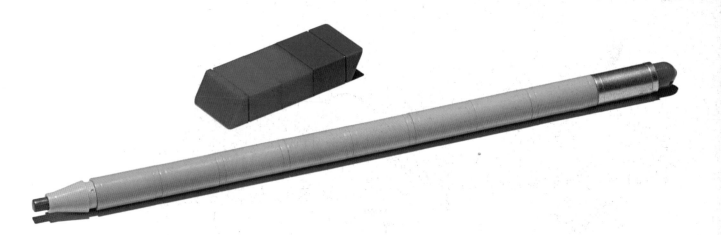

BUMBLEBEE

LEGO models and Transformers have one thing in common: they can change their shape. However, a Transformer is restricted to changing from a vehicle into a robot. By contrast, the possibilities for LEGO models are limitless.

This means that we can of course also reproduce the heroes from the Transformers films. I decided on Bumblebee, mainly because I very much liked the color. The darker yellow (BL: **Bright Light Orange**, Lego shade: Flame Yellowish Orange), which LEGO has been producing since around the year 2000, was at first only used sporadically by LEGO in sets. In recent years, though, it has been used more often in the Friends Sets and the Chima Series. The availability of parts in this color has correspondingly improved.

Alongside the striking dark yellow parts, which represent these individual segments of Bumblebee's bodywork, a large number of gray pieces were also used. In order to represent the alien technology of the Transformer as authentically as possible, I built in plenty of technical-looking elements, which do not, however, have any particular function in the finished model but are purely for decorative effect – also known as "Greebles" among LEGO fans. Incidentally, the gray elements are a mixture of the following colors: light gray (BL: light bluish gray, Lego: medium stone grey), dark gray (BL: dark bluish gray, Lego: dark stone grey), metallic silver (Lego: cool silver, Drum Lacquered), flat silver (Lego: silver metallic), and pearl dark gray (Lego: titanium metallic). This combination was supplemented with golden parts in pearl gold (Lego: warm gold) and metallic gold (Lego: warm gold, Drum Lacquered).

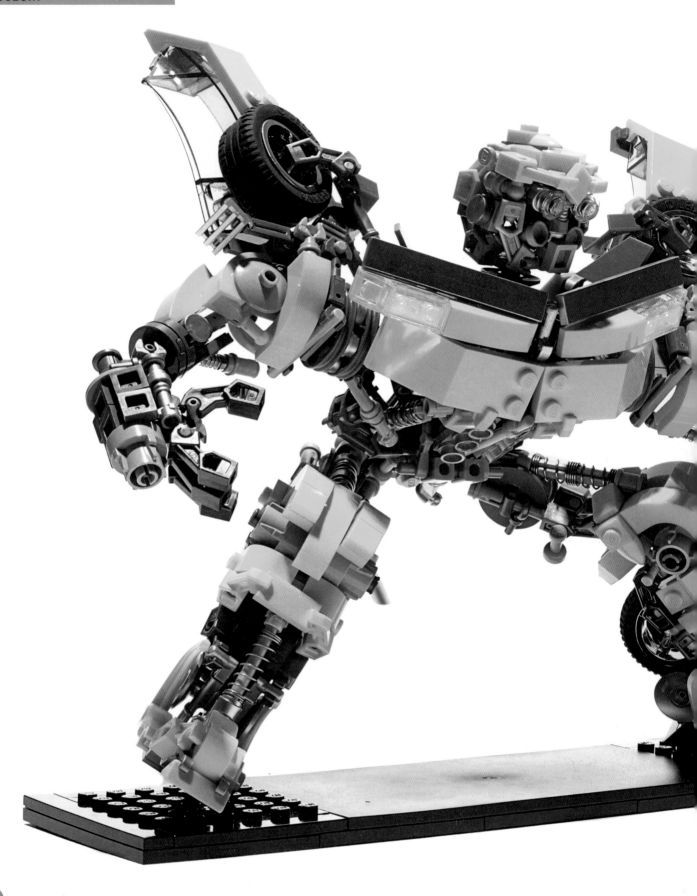

Just as the front of an automobile can become a breastplate for a Transformer, so a LEGO part can also be used outside its actual function, because, as long as you have not used a part, it is only a colored shape waiting to be thrust into the limelight. At the same time, depending on what it is, this part can be connected in different ways. Many have been designed by LEGO with this in mind; others can be found through creativity and plenty of experimentation. The only important thing is that the part should not be damaged. Many of these so-called NPUs have been successful in my MOCs.

Even if you maybe don't see this at first glance, all the elements you can see [below] are used in my Bumblebee. In BrickLink the large piece at the top left is called Motorcycle Chassis (BL: 50859b); it has been used by LEGO in many motorcycles. Because of the technical-looking details and the color (BL:

flat silver, LEGO: silver metallic) it was perfect for my Transformer and has been used in a number of positions, even in the two shoulder joints.

Besides the motorcycle parts, the shoulders also include a Belville crown (BL: Belville, Clothes Crown 72515). It was actually used in Set 5960 of the Belville series to adorn the head of the young king of the sea. Here the crown becomes a wheel rim in a tire. The color is chrome blue, rarely used by LEGO. Even less obvious is the fork (BL: friends accessories cutlery fork 93082i) in Bright Light Orange, which has also found its place in the shoulder. The option envisaged by LEGO for putting the fork into the hand of a figure is not used here. Instead I have taken advantage of the fact that the end is exactly the same width as a stud and thus fits perfectly into the underside of a brick.

Parts already discussed, such as the motorcycle or the Belville crown, can also be found in the foot. A new idea is the use of a special minifig robot arms (BL: arm mechanical 62691), the end of which should actually be inserted in the minifig torso but by chance fits into the existing slot in the motorcycle. Directly above it you can see a spring which, although metal, is still of course an original LEGO part, because LEGO continues to use metal compo-nents in its parts, when conventional ABS isn't suit-able. It's the same with the Technic springs, which come in various strengths (BL: Technic, shock absor-ber 6.5L 731c04, 731c05, and 731c06). Common to all these springs is the fact that they can be pulled apart without doing permanent damage. All you have to do is press the two black ends together. When you have pulled the springs apart, it is easier to use them for details.

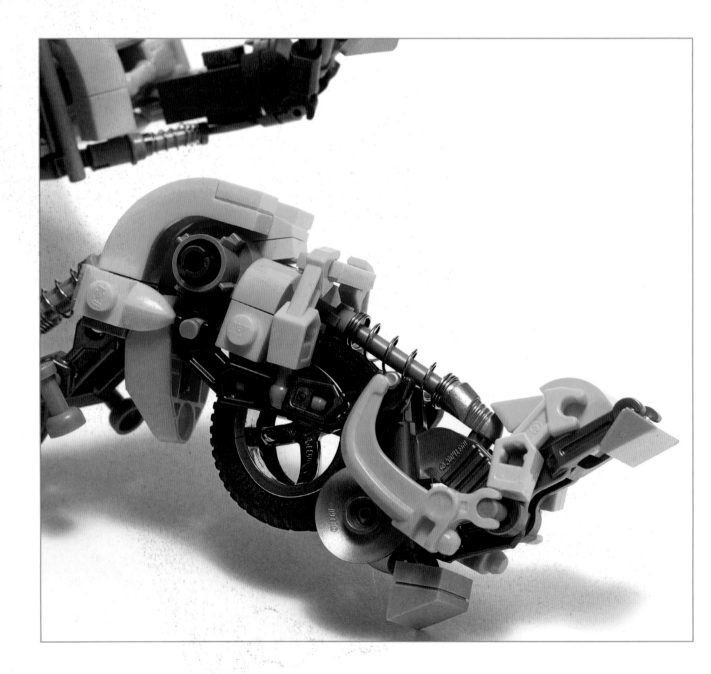

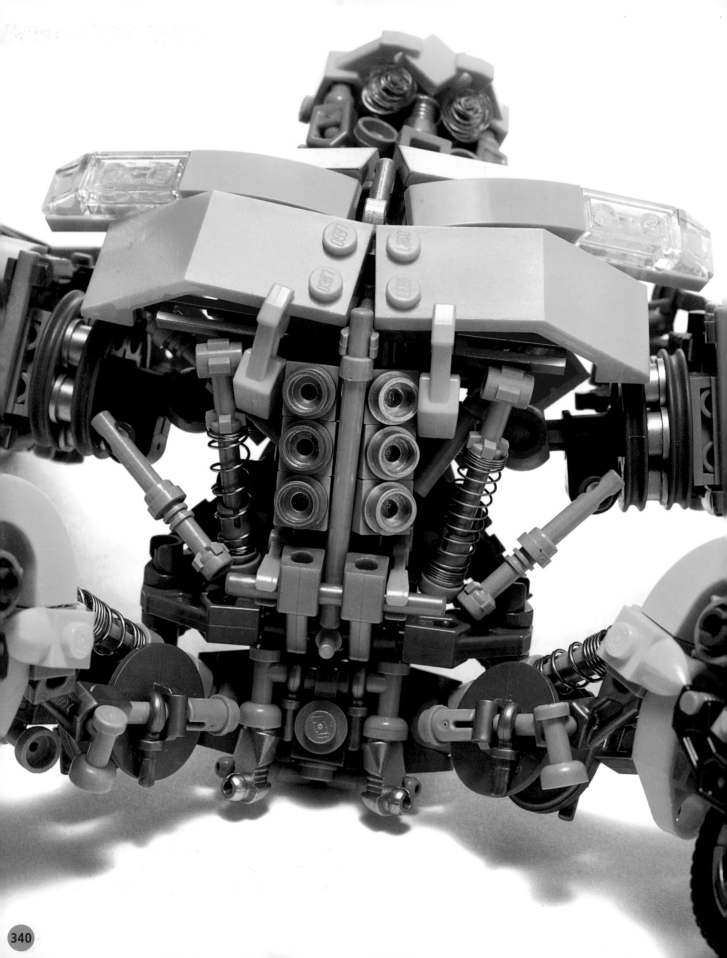

A few interesting pieces are used in Bumblebee's abdomen. Here you will find both the robot arms and the metal springs. A new idea can be discerned in the use of the pirate hook hand (BL: hand pirate hook 2531) in flat silver. Even though the shields (BL: minifig, shield round with stud and ring around edge 91884), which were also used in flat silver, are not illustrated in the picture (on page 337), they are certainly worth a mention.

GASTON TAXI

The old taxi from Gaston Comics, based on a Fiat 509, is modeled here in the typical comic style. The tires are produced using the same technique as the cannons of the Republican gunships, as described in this book (see page 259).

The color **Yellow** should be mentioned in passing here. Thick smoke envelopes the category "Control the action." Something black and orange and a few bits and pieces lying on the ground represent the backfire. For the road surface I first used 1x2 profile bricks (brick, modified 1x2 with masonry profile (brick profile), BL: 98283, LEGO 6000311) to build a wall and then laid it flat. Of course the stickers round about are original LEGO parts.

CAMERAS

If you look more closely at our Tips and Tricks book, you will see that a camera team is busy in the museum taking pictures of the exhibits. I will explain here how the team's camera is put together:

The core of the video camera is an ordinary suitcase for minifigures (minifig, utensil briefcase BL: 4449). The lens consists of a single part that can be easily dismantled from the Soccer Stand (sports minifig stand soccer with spring and green pin, BL: 30488c01). For the tripod we used three long rods (bar 3L, BL: 87994). You can of course use longer rods to give a correspondingly higher tripod. These three rods are inserted from below in the three gaps in the steering wheel (vehicle, steering wheel small, two studs a meter, BL: 30663). To fasten the camera to the lens you take a robot hand (bar 1L with clip mechanical claw, BL: 48729 or 48729b). You can give the camera a second, supplementary lens by placing a Technic box (Technic hub/handle 1x1, BL: 424) on the pin. (Not in the picture, but can be seen on the stills camera on the right.)

There is also a stills camera to be seen in the museum. The tripod is identical to that of the video camera. For the stills camera we used the official LEGO camera (minifig, utensil camera handheld style, BL: 30089 or 30089b), but extended. The lens is a Technic box (see above) and the flash comes from a Technic figure. To get at the part, you have to completely dismantle a Technic figure (for example BL: tech025). First you have to pull the arm out of the torso and divide it into its two segments. With a thin screwdriver you can then press the pin out of the joint, which gives you the elbow joint, which you can then clamp into the underside of the camera. To fasten the stills camera to the lens, you use an open wrench (minifig, utensil tool open end wrench, BL: 6246e).

I have built all the parts in black. If other colors are available, you can of course instal all the parts in alternative colors to make the cameras more individual.

Tip: You can also use the other elements that can be extracted from Technic figures (e.g. the feet) in your own models. Sometimes they enable you to discover entirely new construction techniques!

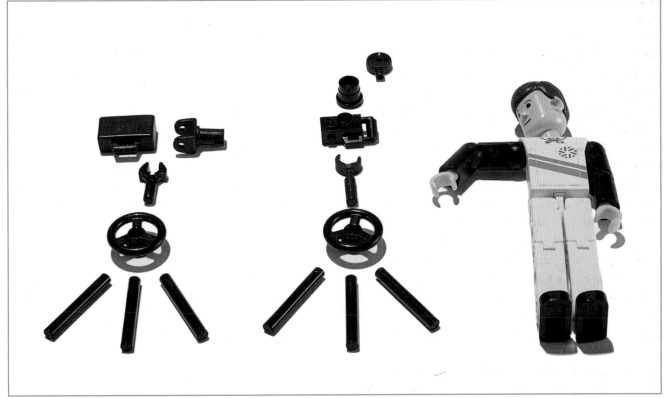

HELICOPTER

As a great fan of unusual colors and parts I decided to build the helicopter (below) from the book "Build Your Own City" in **Olive Green**. This turned out to be easier than expected, even though I first had to consider how I could manage with the few parts available in this color. I used a few parts in dark bluish gray as well. There were two reasons for this. Firstly, it is simply not possible to obtain or improvise all the parts in olive green and, secondly, in my opinion, models in several colors are just more exciting.

LAUREL AND HARDY

Laurel and Hardy accompanied me throughout my childhood. I haven't forgotten the rickety old Model T Fords, and of course I just had to build a version in LEGO at some point! The driver's cab or seat gets its typical form from the use of seats (minifig, utensil seat 2x2, BL: 4079, LEGO 407926) that are built in sideways. The rather sad-looking fir trees that caused so much annoyance in the film Big Business are described as **Green**.

Rubber tires have been pulled over the coach wheels in exactly the same way as shown for the Lanz tractor. And perhaps we should also mention that two disks, one on top of the other, fit into one clip, forming a nice windscreen.

On the other side of the exhibition room we can see the unusual **Dark Turquoise** hands of the chemistry laboratory assistant and a desk in **Sand Blue**. The test tubes are created using the SNOT technique, with Technic bricks embedded in the bench. The microscope looks more difficult than it is. Only the color of the glass plate is not so easy to get hold of. The wheelchair tires are again made from bicycle tires, only this time they are inserted in the holes of clips, which are found on the back.

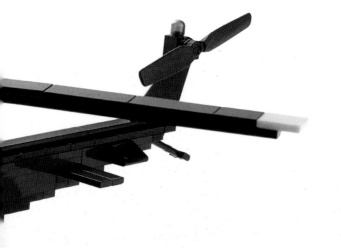

HOT AIR BALLOON

The new pieces from the Friends series (white panel 4x4x13 curved tapered with clip at each end, BL:
18969, LEGO: 6096321) naturally invite you to build
a hot air balloon. But I wanted to build a basket of
my own for it in **Dark Green**.

To make this I used the technique that you can clearly see in the picture [left]. For the sandbags I again
used the sacks made from the Clikits element.

BLUE MAN GROUP

Blue here stands for the Blue Man Group. During this appearance we can demonstrate how you can use different ideas to simulate paint running over. For example, round tiles were simply laid on the floor in front of the platform.

The new version of the Technic connector (Technic, pin connector round 2L with slot (pin joiner round), BL: 62462, LEGO 4526982) has a slit at the side. This means the minifigure can hold the element superbly.

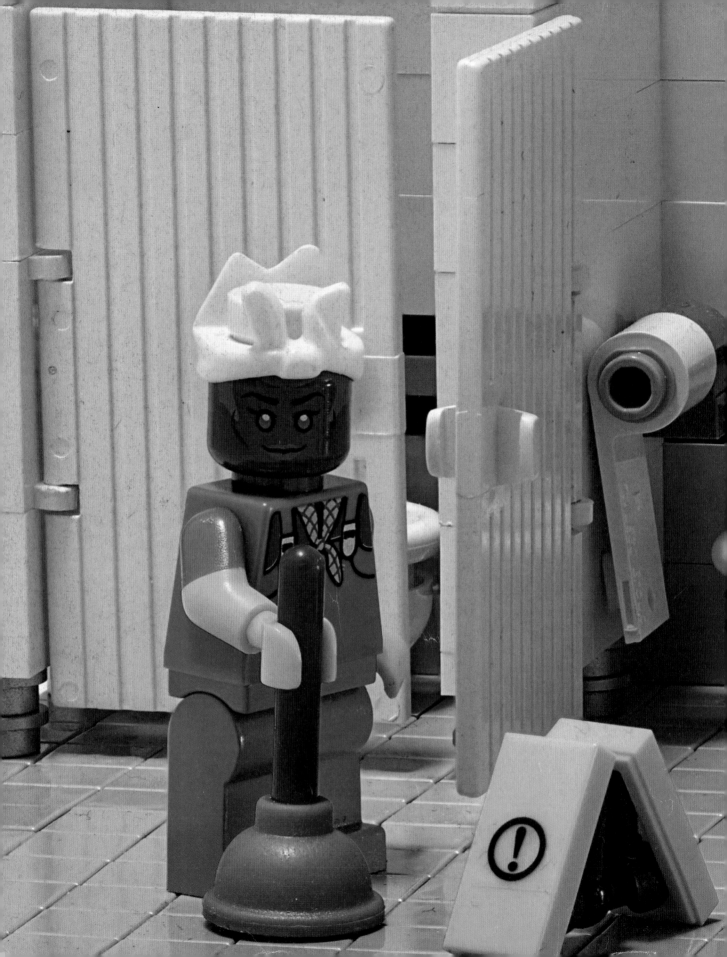

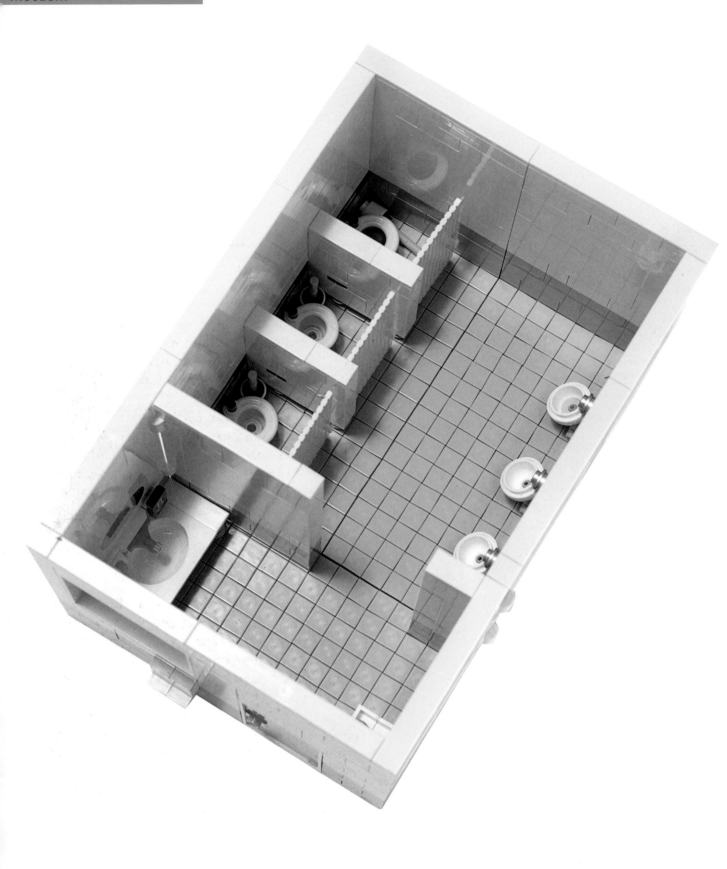

TOILET

We concede that it's a bit decadent to build the toilet in **Maersk Blue**. All the same, I once bought an envelope of 1x1 tiles on spec, so it seemed like a good opportunity to use them.

Our cleaner was inspired by the revue artist Dave Davis. You will have no difficulty in recognizing his headscarf as a reversed neckerchief. The best way to represent unwound toilet paper is a little door – that's an old trick. And don't worry, it's only a chocolate frog sitting in the bowl! The warning notice has a fixture made from a Pneumatic T Piece and two hands. A little bit of homework: just build it!

In the course of the preparations for shooting the photos for this book, this wet area somehow grew into a small stage set. From above you can see the fresh and not so fresh urinals. For these you just use transparent 1x1 round tiles. Can you also spot our favorite cone again?

Jumpers (BL: 3794) half buried in the wall give us the right distance for the paper towel holder. The emergency exit signs in the museum were produced in the same way.

We have used hinges in the walls of our toilet, so that the whole area can be folded up.

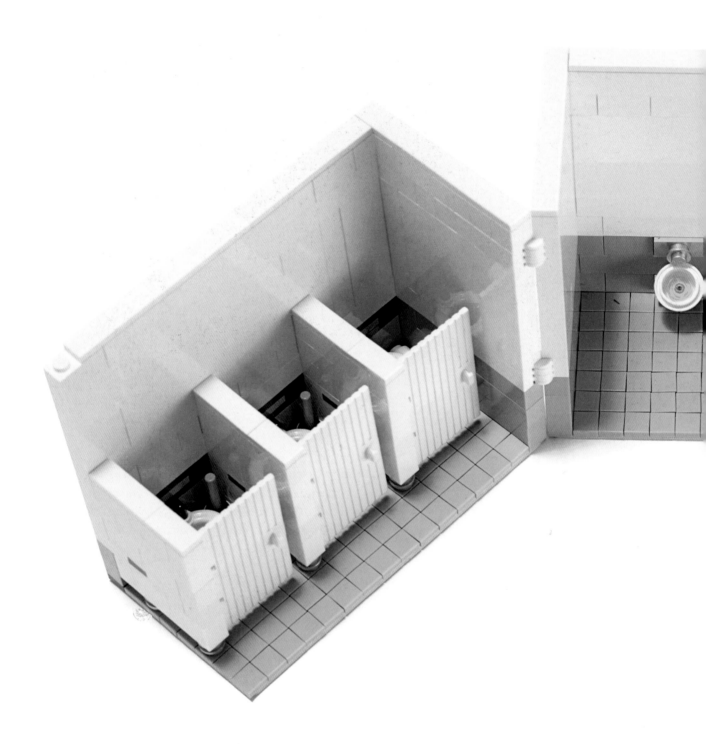

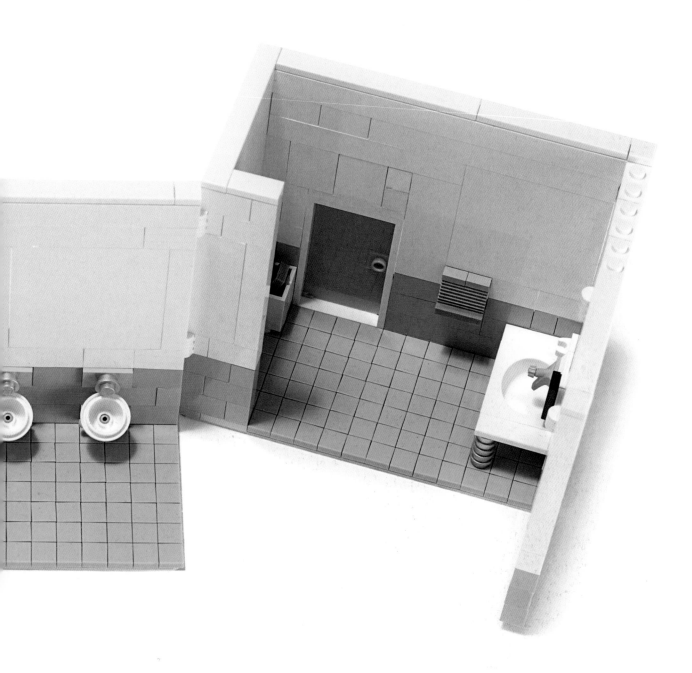

SPACESHIP

Karl and Lars are the two eight-year-old builders of this spaceship in **Blue-Violet** bricks, which resembles a rocket. If you look closely, you can clearly see both of them.
And our photographer Thomas was immediately reproduced for the virtual photo shoot along with the boys.

▌HEART

The round display cases on the right of the previous picture are full of interesting colors. Slowly now, from left to right:

Glow in the Dark Trans: The mask on the floor of the front display case
Trans-Dark Pink: The jumping fish
Trans-Yellow: The starfish on the floor of the front display case

The central and rear display cases contain snakes in **Trans-Dark Blue**, **Trans-Orange**, **Trans-Neon Green**, and **Trans-Purple**.
Our little up-and-coming model builders Karl and Lars have conjured up a heart of **Medium Violet**. The bricks for this only appeared once in a brick replacement pack. And the telephoto lens of the camera is also obtainable in yellow.

42

This gigantic pump in **Sand Purple** was only available in 2001 in the Life on Mars Set: 7317.
So the answer to the question "after life, the universe and all the rest" comes in **Lavender**.

■CANDIES

We show the color **Bright Pink**, once again in a re-alistic way, with the rose-pink licorice. This is made possible by the new inverse tiles (tile, modified 2x2 inverted, BL: 11203).

For the lollipop we reveal a novel fixing method: rubber bands. Technic, axle connector double fle-xible (rubber), BL: 45590, LEGO: 4198367. You can see exactly how it works from the exploded photo.

■TRAFFIC LIGHT MEN

The green traffic light man in **Trans-Green** consists almost entirely of wedges, almost all of which are simply clamped in. For translucent elements it is sensible to tile the transition from thick to transparent parts, so that the studs aren't visible in the transparent bricks.
The red traffic light man demonstrates the color **Trans-Red**.
If you look carefully, you will realize that the entire traffic light men picture is built into the white wall rotated through 90°.

ICE SCULPTURE

Not everyone can create ice sculptures with a power saw. With LEGO it's a bit easier. Grab your **Trans-Clear** collection and start building.

The scrubbing brush in the background is made from a rotated 1x3 tile and has no permanent connection with the handle – but it works all the same!

In the front you can see another Yellowish Green element: the little boy's balloon.

GIANT HGV RC EVENT

A further attraction for children is the giant HGV RC Event. Hopefully the truck in **Flat Silver** won't drive into the wall. On this double page there is a lot more still to discover; just have a good look!

STELES

These columns in **Light Blue** don't just grow out of the ground, or do they?

▎WELL

A well as a work of art – far too expensive in **Chrome Silver**. There are just 100 different elements in this color, including such items as arms, slopes, plates, and helmets.

▎BLUE BALL

For everyone who is now wondering what this funny ball is doing on the following pages: it's an official part! It first appeared in Set 8269 "Cyber Stinger" in 1999 (BL: 41250 in Blue, LEGO: 4100758 or also Duplo Ball for Ball Tube BL: 23065, LEGO: 4100758).

Although the base doesn't contain any particularly rare elements, it has an extremely interesting color by the name of **Speckle Black-Silver**. Many people may know this color from the LEGO Viking or Castle sets.

Unfortunately there are no exhibits available for the following colors. However, we wanted to give them at least a brief mention for the sake of completeness:

Glitter Trans-Neon Green
Glitter Trans-Light Blue
Glitter Trans-Purple
Pearl Very Light Gray
Pearl White
Speckle Dark Bluish Gray-Silver
Copper

Color	BrickLink name	LEGO name	Produced in years	Book page
	White	White	1950–2015	268
	Very Light Gray	Light Grey	1997–2006	282
	Very Light Bluish Gray	Light Stone Grey	2004–2013	282
	Light Bluish Gray	Medium Stone Grey	2003–2015	289
	Light Gray	Grey	1954–2008	290
	Dark Gray	Dark Grey	1961–2007	290
	Dark Bluish Gray	Dark Stone Grey	2003–2015	294
	Black	Black	1957–2015	288
	Dark Red	Dark Red	1961–2015	296
	Red	Bright Red	1950–2015	301
	Rust	Rust	1989–2001	282
	Salmon	Medium Red	1997–2003	303
	Light Salmon	Light Red	1997–2004	282
	Sand Red	Sand Red	2001–2004	306
	Reddish Brown	Reddish Brown	2003–2015	309
	Brown	Earth Orange	1974–2006	282
	Dark Brown	Dark Brown	2008–2015	312
	Dark Tan	Sand Yellow	1961–2015	294
	Tan	Brick Yellow	1958–2015	314
	Light Flesh	Light Nougat	2003–2015	323
	Flesh	Nougat	1979–2015	318
	Medium Dark Flesh	Medium Nougat	2010–2015	324

Color	BrickLink name	LEGO name	Produced in years	Book page
	Dark Flesh	Brown	2004–2006	282
	Fabuland Brown	Brick Red	1979–1997	297
	Fabuland Orange	Light Brown	1985–1989	282
	Earth Orange	Light Orange Brown	1982–2006	318
	Dark Orange	Dark Orange	1979–2015	289
	Orange	Bright Orange	1993–2015	328
	Medium Orange	Bright Yellowish Orange	1950–2013	318
	Bright Light Orange	Flame Yellowish Orange	2000–2015	330
	Light Orange	Medium Yellowish Orange	1998–2005	307
	Very Light Orange	Light Yellowish Orange	2000–2000	282
	Dark Yellow	Curry	2004–2005	322
	Yellow	Bright Yellow	1950–2015	342
	Bright Light Yellow	Cool Yellow	2003–2015	282
	Light Yellow	Light Yellow	1994–2011	324
	Light Lime	Light Yellowish Green	1992–2007	282
	Yellowish Green	Spring Yellowish Green	2012–2015	282
	Medium Lime	Medium Yellowish Green	1998–2005	303
	Lime	Bright Yellowish Green	1982–2015	323
	Olive Green	Olive Green	2012–2015	348
	Dark Green	Earth Green	1961–2015	354
	Green	Dark Green	1950–2015	353
	Bright Green	Bright Green	1950–2015	318

Color	BrickLink name	LEGO name	Produced in years	Book page
	Medium Green	Medium Green	1950–2004	282
	Light Green	Light Green	1992–2007	300
	Sand Green	Sand Green	1964–2015	282
	Dark Turquoise	Bright Bluish Green	1998–2015	352
	Light Turquoise	Medium Bluish Green	1998–2004	282
	Aqua	Light Bluish Green	1998–2006	282
	Light Aqua	Aqua	2011–2015	322
	Dark Blue	Earth Blue	1961–2015	312
	Blue	Bright Blue	1950–2015	356
	Dark Azure	Dark Azure	2000–2015	303
	Medium Azure	Medium Azure	2012–2015	312
	Medium Blue	Medium Blue	1950–2015	313
	Maersk Blue	Pastel Blue	1974–2011	358
	Bright Light Blue	Light Royal Blue	2004–2015	318
	Light Blue	Light Blue	1950–2007	384
	Sky Blue	Dove Blue	2003–2007	282
	Sand Blue	Sand Blue	2001–2015	352
	Blue-Violet	Royal Blue	2004–2005	364
	Dark Blue-Violet	Dark Royal Blue	2004–2006	282
	Violet	Medium Bluish Violet	1992–2004	322
	Medium Violet	Lilac	1999–2005	367
	Light Violet	Light Bluish Violet	1994–2004	282

Color	BrickLink name	LEGO name	Produced in years	Book page
	Dark Purple	Medium Lilac	2003–2015	288
	Purple	Bright Violet	1996–2008	282
	Light Purple	Bright Reddish Lilac	2004–2007	318
	Medium Lavender	Medium Lavender	2012–2015	282
	Lavender	Lavender	2011–2015	371
	Sand Purple	Sand Violet	2001–2002	370
	Magenta	Bright Reddish Violet	2000–2015	318
	Dark Pink	Medium Reddish Violet	1994–2015	318
	Medium Dark Pink	Pink	1992–1996	282
	Bright Pink	Light Purple	2003–2015	372
	Pink	Light Reddish Violet	1991–2006	282
	Light Pink	Light Pink	1994–2007	302
	Trans-Clear	Transparent	1950–2015	379
	Trans-Black	Transparent Brown	1999–2015	300
	Trans-Red	Transparent Red	1969–2015	374
	Trans-Neon Orange	Tranparent Fluorescent Reddish Orange	1993–2015	318
	Trans-Orange	Transparent Bright Orange	2003–2015	366
	Trans-Neon Yellow	Transparent Fluorescent Yellow	2001–2005	318
	Trans-Yellow	Transparent Yellow	1969–2015	366
	Trans-Neon Green	Transparent Fluorescent Green	1990–2015	366
	Trans-Bright Green	Transparent Bright Yellowish Green	2003–2015	286
	Trans-Green	Transparent Green	1969–2015	374

Color	BrickLink name	LEGO name	Produced in years	Book page
	Trans-Dark Blue	Transparent Blue	1978–2015	366
	Trans-Medium Blue	Transparent Fluorescent Blue	2001–2015	318
	Trans-Light Blue	Transparent Light Blue	1985–2015	290
	Trans-Very Light Blue	Transparent Light Bluish Green	2003–2006	282
	Trans-Light Purple	Transparent Reddish Lilac	2005–2006	282
	Trans-Purple	Transparent Bright Bluish Violet	2000–2015	366
	Trans-Dark Pink	Transparent Fluorescent Red	1998–2015	282
	Trans-Pink	Transparent Bright Purple	2003–2006	282
	Chrome Gold	Metalized Gold	1989–2015	306
	Chrome Silver	Metalized Silver	1966–2015	386
	Chrome Antique Brass	Antique Gold	2001–2005	282
	Chrome Black		2009–2009	306
	Chrome Blue	Bluenetal	1998–2006	282
	Chrome Green		1999–1999	286
	Chrome Red		2011	307
	Chrome Pink		2001–2007	282
	Pearl White	Metallic White	2003–2006	387
	Pearl Very Light Gray	Light Grey Metallic	2002–2003	387
	Pearl Light Gray	Cool Silver	1993–2013	324
	Flat Silver	Silver Metallic	1998–2015	380
	Pearl Dark Gray	Titanium Metallic	2002–2015	324
	Metal Blue	Sand Blue Metallic	2002–2006	306

Color	BrickLink name	LEGO name	Produced in years	Book page
	Pearl Light Gold	Gold	2000–2006	306
	Pearl Gold	Warm Gold	2002–2015	324
	Flat Dark Gold	Sand Yellow Metallic	2003–2007	282
	Copper	Copper	2001–2012	387
	Metallic Silver	Cool Silver, Drum Lacquered	1957–2015	302
	Metallic Green		2001–2003	282
	Metallic Gold	Warm Gold, Drum Lacquered / Gold Metalized / Gold Laquered	1997–2015	324
	Milky White	Nature	1963–2008	296
	Glow In Dark White	White Glow	2012–2015	282
	Glow In Dark Opaque	Phosphorescent White	1990–2011	282
	Glow In Dark Trans	Phosphorescent Green	2005–2011	366
	Glitter Trans-Clear	Transparent with Glitter	1999–2015	282
	Glitter Trans-Neon Green	Transparent Fluorescent Green with Glitter	2015–2015	387
	Glitter Trans-Light Blue	Transparent Light Blue with Glitter	2015–2015	387
	Glitter Trans-Purple	Transparent Bluish Violet (Glitter)	2000–2015	387
	Glitter Trans-Dark Pink	Transparent Pink Glitter / Transparent Medium Reddish Violet Glitter	1999–2012	282
	Speckle Black-Silver	Cool Silver, Diffuse	2005–2013	388
	Speckle Black-Gold		2010–2011	324
	Speckle Black-Copper	Copper, Diffuse	2006–2006	324
	Speckle Dark Bluish Gray-Silver		2006–2006	387

STICKERS

Stickers can be used to enhance many things. After all, LEGO encloses a sticker book with almost every second set. Even when you have used all the motifs, you shouldn't get rid of the remainder. There are often colored strips left over that you can still use in some way. Or maybe just the background color. There are also letters and numbers printed on the edge of each sheet, and there's always something you can use them for.

A few examples:

I had actually only kept sticker sheet 62318 (Set 7586) so that at some point I could cut out chrome strips for cars from it. In fact I also used it for a flower symbol for King Arthur.

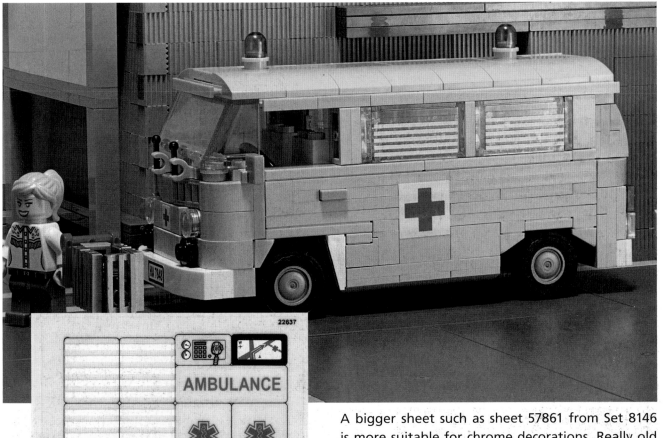

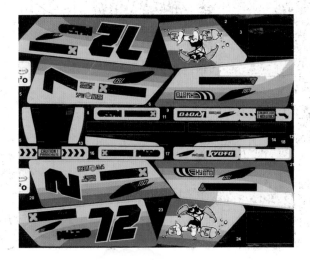

A bigger sheet such as sheet 57861 from Set 8146 is more suitable for chrome decorations. Really old Red Cross stickers came in handy for this Red Cross VW Bulli. Also, the white stripes for the windows come from sheet 199699, which didn't actually come from a set, but was enclosed with building book 250. However, the white stripes still appear occasionally now, for example on sheet 14082 (Set 60023).

22637

AMBULANCE

POLICE

POLICE

POLICE

X TREME

14082/6035463 © 2013 LEGO GROUP

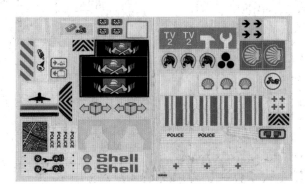

Printed colors on a transparent background are a great favorite of mine, for example the wood grain of sheet 92948 (Set 4840). Then you can select the color of the wood underneath. Transparent stickers often accompanied Exo Force.

One peculiarity: in the middle of sheet 54907 (Set 7700) is an exclamation mark!

For the VW Police Bus I have even found German characters on sheet 52800 (Set 7245). For the Bulli version of the city emergency vehicles you again need stripes, which can be found on sheet 64949 (Set 7685).

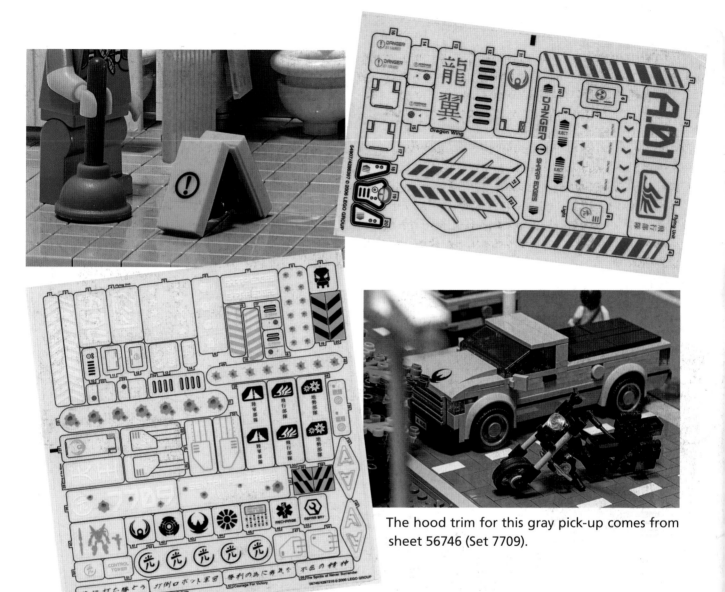

The hood trim for this gray pick-up comes from sheet 56746 (Set 7709).

Captain America's star from sheet 10867 (Set 6865) now decorates the old police vehicle.

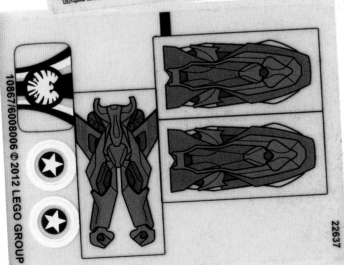

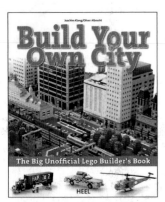
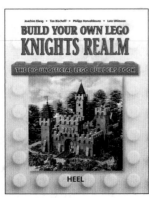
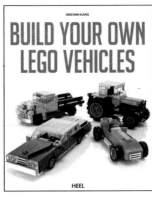